Optimizing Bank Relations

Managing Costs and Services

Kenneth L. Parkinson

TIS Publishing

Hopewell, NJ

Published by:
Treasury Information Services
P.O. Box 99
Hopewell, NJ 08525

Orders:
Tel: 888-TIS-BOOK
Fax: 609-466-0091
www.tisconsulting.com

Published 2005
Printed in the United States of America
ISBN 0-9633680-8-7

Table of Contents

About the Author

Kenneth L. Parkinson

Kenneth Parkinson is a managing director with Treasury Information Services and a visiting professor of finance at NYU's Stern School of Business in New York City. He is an experienced consultant, educator, writer, and financial manager.

His experience as a consultant and as a corporate treasury manager has included development and implementation of major treasury systems in both mainframe and PC environments. As a treasury manager, he evaluated and selected treasury services from commercial and investment banks and other providers worldwide.

As a treasury consultant, he has worked closely with clients to conduct treasury "audit" reviews, select appropriate banking services, evaluate bank service charges, and design effective treasury systems. He has provided advisory services to major commercial banks to help in assessing market acceptance of new products and in solving current customer problems.

As an educator, Mr. Parkinson teaches undergraduate and graduate courses in finance. He also has designed and served as course leader for the American Management Association's courses in cash and treasury management.

Ken Parkinson has authored, co-authored or made major contributions to more than a dozen books on cash management, including *Preparing for Cash Management Certification, How to Prepare an RFP for Treasury Services, Managing Bank Relations, Corporate Liquidity, Cash Management Templates, Essentials of Cash Management*

(2nd and 3rd eds.), and *Treasury Manager's Guide to the Internet*. He has served as editor-in-chief of the *Journal of Cash Management*, technology editor and contributing editor with *Corporate Cashflow* magazine, senior editor with *Business Credit* magazine, and co-editor *of The Treasury Pro*, a monthly newsletter.

Ken Parkinson holds a BS degree from The Pennsylvania State University and an MBA degree in international business from the Wharton Graduate School of Business at the University of Pennsylvania. He was part of the team that first developed the CCM exam and is a permanently certified cash manager.

Preface

More than ten years ago, I wrote *Managing Bank Relations*. It was, I believe, the first book ever to focus solely on this subject. Much has happened in the world of banking relations since 1991—the growth of the Web, e-commerce, multi-state bank mergers, and technological advancement—to name a few of the changes. So, I feel an update is due.

As I planned this book and assessed what the "state of the art" is in managing bank relations, I was amazed to find how much had *not* changed. I also found that many treasury managers still failed to give bank relationship management much time in their "to-do" items.

I think that managing bank relations actively, objectively, and efficiently should be included as one of the "best practices" in treasury management. I have always believed that managing bank relations effectively pays dividends to an organization. Do it right, and your organization can benefit from cost-effective services. Do it wrong— or not at all—and you your company is losing money, month after month after month.

This book is intended to be a "good read" for cash managers and for bankers, as well. It doesn't matter at what your level of experience is. Beginners, experienced cash managers, and bankers will find something in this book to help them do their job a little better.

Kenneth L. Parkinson
Hopewell, New Jersey
August 2004

Acknowledgments

I would like to thank Larry Forman, partner, Ernst & Young for permission to use data from the annual cash management survey Ernst and Young conducts with the major banks. I would also like to thank Richard Richardson, senior vice president, Phoenix-Hecht, for allowing me to use information from the *Phoenix- Hecht Blue Book of Bank Prices* and for providing an additional review of the book manuscript.

No author can edit and publish a book by himself. In my case, this book would not have been possible without the editorial and publishing skills of my partner, Joyce Ochs. She has provided invaluable editing, review, layout, and countless other services. Her insights and efforts have truly shaped the final book. Finally, heartfelt thanks to Susan Ochs for her superb copy editing and proofreading of the manuscript.

Disclaimer

The author and the publisher have used their best efforts in preparing this book to provide accurate information. It is sold with the understanding that the publisher and the author are not engaged in rendering legal, accounting, or other professional services. If legal or other expert assistance is required, the services of a competent professional should be sought.

Every effort has been made to make this book as complete and as accurate as possible. However, there may be mistakes, both typographical and in content. Furthermore, the information in this book is current only up to the printing date.

The author and the publisher shall have neither liability nor responsibility to any person or entity with respect to any loss or damage caused, or alleged to have been caused, directly or indirectly, by the information in this book.

If you do not wish to be bound by the above, you may return this book to the publisher for a full refund.

1

It's a New Ball Game

For many years, organizations and their banks looked at their relationship as a long-term commitment of mutual loyalty. However, this view of things no longer holds, due to a number of developments that I shall discuss in this book.

If you think the old rules still apply, you're sadly mistaken. Managing bank relations—the establishment, maintenance, and elimination of credit and non-credit services—is viewed differently today. This change applies across the board from small companies to large multinational corporations to not-for-profit organizations to governmental entities.

The influence of credit needs

In the past, it was convenient to think of the relationship as a partnership, although I never fully subscribed to this point of view. Many organizations found themselves with dozens of bank relationships or even more, if they had retail locations. It was natural for one or two banks to become the "leaders of the pack," while the others played subordinate roles.

Customers frequently showed loyalty to the bank or banks that fulfilled their credit needs, and the credit relationship heavily

influenced the choice of banks. Banks were focused on the revenue generated by credit activity, and this focus often dominated
the bank's point of view.

Years ago, a strong credit need often dictated how a company looked at its banks. For instance, a company with sizable
credit needs might spread the business among several banks to
obtain the amount of credit it required. On the other hand, if one
bank could fill that credit need, it could expect additional non-
credit services as added business because credit needs were so
valuable and non-credit needs were not considered separately.

Changes in bank use

As treasury managers began to recognize that their cash management needs were growing and that they could tap the commercial paper market for short-term credit needs, they started handling credit and non-credit services separately. They began to select the bank or banks that could provide the best non-credit
services, independent of credit needs.

At the start of the 21st century, interest rates were at historically low levels, and this encouraged banks to focus on their profitable lines of business. This meant non-credit services, where the
banks themselves could set and reset the prices. The thin spreads
on credit services were not likely to provide revenues the way
cash management (non-credit) services could.

In my original book on this subject, *Managing Bank Relations*,
I talked a lot about lead banks and why banks coveted that spot.
Being the lead bank usually translated into a substantial amount
of business for the bank in terms of credit and non-credit services.
The lead bank did whatever it took to keep its lead customers
happy, matching other services as needed or solving a customer's
special problems, such as moving funds to a difficult foreign site
or arranging for emergency funding quickly. Although this arrangement created strong loyalties, it was also subject to market
pressures.

As companies and the banking world underwent consolidation, both customers and banks began to reassess how bank services should be viewed. Banking was changing. With the growth
of a handful of major banks through merger and new legislative

freedom, the close relationship between customer and bank was being replaced by a more impersonal one.

From partner to service provider

Customers had long shed excessive compensating bank balances to fees for service charges, just as banks had shifted their focus from garnering balances to generating desirable fee-based income. As banks and companies focused on fees, they changed from partners to service providers and users. Banking service charges have risen sharply over the past decade, and the changeover to a service provider environment seems virtually complete.

As a result of changes in bank and customer attitudes toward banking services, bank relationship management has changed. It seems more appropriate for you to consider your bank as a critical service provider with whom you need to maintain a healthy buyer-seller relationship, similar to what develops between an organization and its other long-time suppliers.

You need to function in this regard as a purchasing manager because that is what you are—a purchasing manager for bank-provided services. Familiarity and closeness are still related to the provision of services, but they are not the common goal of two linked parties (as is the case in a partnership).

Overview

Managing bank relations is one of your most important responsibilities as a treasury manager. It is one of the most common responsibilities of all treasury managers, no matter what their title or executive level. It is often misunderstood or taken for granted. Nevertheless, if conducted properly and effectively, maintaining effective bank relations pays dividends for your company.

You may believe that strong bank relations are only important if your organization is a borrower. The last few years have shown that this is not the case.

While treasury managers have experienced a strong push from their bankers for non-credit services if credit services are needed, organizations that are primarily investors have felt similar pressure from their banks for more non-credit services. These companies have seen more attractive investment rates and om their cash management banks than from other banks where u.ey have maintained a relationship but few services.

Historically, commercial banks have played a major role in the development of treasury management practices. They have been educators, consultants, service developers, and service providers.

To ensure that their organizations receive appropriate banking services, treasury managers are continually involved with their banks. This activity, above all others, is one that treasury managers never relinquish completely as they scale the career ladder. I believe that managing bank relations actually takes on more importance for senior treasury and corporate financial executives.

In this chapter, I will discuss the role of bank relations and how this activity fits in the overall framework of the corporate treasury function. In tracing its historical importance and the changes in approach, we will establish the appropriate perspective for the more detailed discussions that follow in later chapters.

Market pressures

Over time, the corporate-banking relationship has grown to become a big business. There are several groups that periodically investigate the market for cash management and credit services.

Two of the more well-known groups are the public accounting/consulting firm of Ernst & Young (E&Y), which conducts an annual study of market size through its New York office, and Phoenix-Hecht (Research Triangle Park, NC), which conducts surveys of various market segments. Phoenix-Hecht also publishes the *Blue Book of Bank Prices*, which shows the changes in bank service charges from year to year for individual charges or components of service charges. Figure 1-1 shows the results for the E&Y study and Phoenix-Hecht studies for 1999-2004.

Although the overall market size is an impressive figure, Figure 1-1 shows that the rate of growth, as measured by E&Y, has slowed in recent years. The data show that banks reported a growth rate in 2002 of 1.5%, down sharply from 6.5% in the previous year, but expected to rebound to a 5% rate in 2003 (actual figures were not available before this book was printed). Even 5% is lower than the rates for 1999 (7%) and 2000 (6.0%).

The E&Y study attributes the slowing growth rate to the slowly recovering economy and low interest rate environment. According to E&Y's latest survey, commercial banks collect more than $12 billion annually through the provision of non-credit (cash management) services to corporations.

The Phoenix-Hecht figures show a different picture. According to the *Blue Book*, bank service charges have shown a generally increasing trend, although not as steep as the rate for 1999-2001 reported in the E&Y study. Unlike the E&Y numbers, the *Blue Book* does not show a distinct decrease in charges for 2002. As the figure shows, the Phoenix-Hecht numbers have been consistently lower than E&Y's figures until 2002-2003, when they are close.

Figure 1-1: Growth Rate of Cash Management Market

Year	Growth Rate[1]	Price Increase[2]
1999	7.0%	1.7%
2000	6.0%	3.0%
2001	6.5%	3.3%
2002	1.5%	4.9%
2003	5.0% (est.)	4.3%

Sources: [1] *Ernst & Young 20th Cash Management Survey*
[2] *Phoenix-Hecht Blue Book of Bank Prices (2003-2004)*

What can explain this discrepancy? One could be the difference in sources – E&Y gets its input directly from the top banks, including all of the top 20 bank holding companies and almost 90% of the top 50. Phoenix-Hecht uses voluntary submissions of account analysis statements from more than 1,000 companies, and its data are based on price changes in the 56 services covered in the survey. In describing the survey methodology, Phoenix-Hecht notes that the survey includes the "17 largest banks in terms of cash management activity." The description also notes that these banks earned more than $5 billion in revenues from cash management services.

I think we can attribute the slowing growth rate to several factors:

- *Steady competition among banks for a saturated market*
  The number of new organizations purchasing services in significant quantities has been steadily decreasing. Even with increased use by smaller organizations, the overall potential revenue is not likely to change substantially.

- *Consolidation of bank relationships*
  Organizations, especially larger ones, have continued to reduce the number of banks they use, eliminating duplicate or excessive services, and reducing the overall revenues to banks.

- *More infrequent price increases than in past years*
  Banks may be "locked in" to smaller increases by market pressures and increased use by organizations of price-controlling approaches, such as requests for proposal.

- *"Commodity" shopping*
  Many organizations have become indifferent when it comes to basic banking services, looking for cheaper prices for such services. These are the non-value-added buyers.

- *Large corporate market saturation*
  By now, many observers feel that the high end of the market—large corporations—have most of the products and services they need, so there really is not any new business. This condition leads to lower prices or slower growth as these buyers *price shop* for mature cash management services.

Has there been a buyer's market for cash management services? Many banks have felt the pressure of competition in responding to requests for proposal from their customers; they might conclude that the buyers have a great deal of choice. However, many treasury managers might disagree, as they have experienced increasing service charges despite their use of competitive bidding approaches.

The E&Y survey found that banks have been making less money from their large customers. Their revenue growth has come from smaller organizations, many of which seem to be value-added shoppers more than commodity shoppers (according to the survey findings).

Reviewing these items, we can see that many of them are linked to the changing nature of bank relations. Evidence of this is the increased use by treasury managers of the request-for-proposal (RFP) process for new bank service providers. Never before have so many formal RFPs been issued by organizations for their basic cash management services. RFPs have become accepted by treasury managers and banks as the way to select bank services. (I'll discuss RFPs later, in Chapter 7.)

External forces

Corporate needs have not changed substantially in the past ten years or so, but they have been affected by a number of external forces. The merger and acquisition activities among corporations and commercial banks have left their mark in the form of fewer major cash management service providers and fewer corporate users of those services. Much more effort has been put into managing fewer bank relations more effectively in the last decade than ever before.

Furthermore, corporate treasury managers may be rethinking whether it makes sense to keep credit and non-credit banks separate. The bundling of bank service needs may be making a comeback.

One other external force that can greatly affect corporate-bank relationships is regulatory change. The Federal Reserve (Fed) in its role as regulator of U.S. commercial banks can have a substantial impact on company treasury practices.

While most changes from the Fed affect the banks directly, many of these effects also have an impact on corporate-bank relationships. For instance, the Fed substantially reduced the amount of excess float in the banking system during the 1980's. This in turn diminished the importance of bank services designed to take advantage of that float (e.g., disbursing from remote locations). The effect was to consolidate the number of banks a company used because there was no advantage in maintaining bank relationships with specialized disbursing banks. I'll discuss the regulatory influences in a later section in this chapter.

The Broadening Market

For banks faced with a nearly saturated market for the big payers–large corporate customers–the question has been: How can they increase business? The answer has been to probe downward in company size for potential cash management service users.

Bank focus on middle market companies has increased significantly in recent times. Banks may differ on their definition of the middle market segment, but I'll define it as those organizations with annual sales of $10 million to $250 million.

This widening of the corporate market means that more treasury managers will be actively managing their bank relations. Newcomers can learn quickly because there are far more sources than ever before. Bankers will find that these newcomers take less for granted than their predecessors but will still go through the same learning process. They may also be more inclined to pay more attention to price and service and care less about maintaining "the relationship."

Banks as educators

Treasury managers have historically used their bank contacts to keep up-to-date with new technology developments and to obtain information on the "hot" issues that could affect them. Banks take this educational role seriously.

Even though there are non-banking groups (e.g., the national and regional treasury associations) that play leading roles in educating treasury managers, banks can have more impact through their direct marketing and in-person calling efforts. The banks also are the major supporters (financially and otherwise) of the educational forums, and this increases their role as educators of treasury managers.

It makes good marketing sense for the banks to support regional and national meetings because they use these forums to transfer knowledge about new products to potential users and to establish an image among these possible service purchasers. They also use the meetings for more informal contacts with their customers, and these sessions build the overall corporate-bank relationship. Treasury managers rely on their major bank (or banks) for efficient, cost-effective services and timely advice.

Banks as external staff

Bank services may be more than just stand-alone products, however. If you are like many treasury managers in fast-growing smaller or mid-sized companies, you know that you are more likely to use bank services as a way to extend your treasury staff than are larger corporations that have the "luxury" of more full-time treasury players. Middle market companies have molded effective relationships with their banks and use their banks' expertise in many ways.

The reliance on the banks increases the importance of maintaining effective bank relations, and treasury managers in these companies and their bankers readily acknowledge this. For the relationship to work, however, it must be a two-way street.

Bankers must not be reluctant to discuss operating or financial problems with treasury managers, and they must help customers identify and rectify inefficient practices and service misuse. Treasury managers, on the other hand, must be committed to making the most out of bank meetings and to keeping their bankers well informed about their needs and about developments in their companies. Banks can provide help when it's needed, but this requires preparation, time, and effort from both "sides of the desk."

Regulatory and Legislative Changes

Changes in regulations and new legislation have had substantial impact on the corporate-bank relationship. For example, before the Monetary Control Act (1980), companies and banks created elaborate networks to maximize check (disbursement) float by finding faraway locations on which checks were drawn. These remote locations became attractive offerings by some banks and were readily accepted and used by companies that wanted additional days in float. Although the law empowered the Federal Reserve to eliminate remote disbursing, the practice survived in a slightly different form—controlled disbursing.

Banks realized that many companies were interested in something other than the extra float. They wanted information about their daily check clearings on the same day that the checks were to be posted to their accounts.

Banks still use distant branches or affiliates to provide controlled disbursing, but this is to be able to assure that checks drawn on controlled disbursement points will all clear through the Fed. The Fed acknowledges these points and may designate such points for an additional clearing under its High Dollar Group Sort program. Under this program, the Fed transmits clearing totals twice daily to the banks, which, in turn, retransmit the data to their corporate controlled disbursement customers.

Bank and company cooperation

Changes to the Fed's regulations can also affect bank relations. For instance, when the Fed announced its intentions to eliminate daylight overdrafts created by banks, treasury managers were justifiably concerned about the impact of the new regulations on their ability to move funds easily. It seemed possible that an organization might not be able to move funds even though it had them in its account because its bank was over its overdraft limit.

While this transfer "gridlock" has not materialized to any great extent, the possibility did make many of the organizations take a good look at their banks' financial conditions and consider shifting their business to other banks that appeared to have more room in their limits. The important point to note here is that the perception of a problem caused a great deal of consternation between companies and their banks and could have resulted in major shifts in business from banks considered weaker to those considered stronger. This issue also showed how banks and companies can discuss issues together and express their opinions to regulatory agencies like the Fed.

Same-day presentment was another issue that had potential ramifications for bank relations. The Fed announced that it was considering changing the rules about how and when checks could be presented for clearance. Initially the deadline was very liberal, extending well into the business day.

As was the case with daylight overdrafts, the banks and their customers worked together to understand the potential impact of later check presentment. It appeared that later presentment would virtually eliminate the timing that enabled banks to offer controlled disbursement services, probably the most popular cash management service for companies and a profitable one for banks.

Companies and banks alike responded so negatively that there is no doubt the feedback convinced the Fed to allow banks (and companies) to protect the valued service. It also showed how effective banks and customers working together can be.

The Association for Financial Professionals (AFP), which represents treasury managers from most of the largest and from many of the middle market companies, also played an important role in facilitating the interchange between banks and companies and between companies and the Fed. Formed in the late 1970's, the association has established a significant presence in Washington and actively monitors the Fed and the Congress on issues that could affect how companies handle their treasury activities.

The impact of regulatory change

For more than half of the 20th century, efficient bank relations were stifled by legislation designed to prevent the financial disasters of the Depression years from recurring. Barred from most financial transactions having to do with the issuance of stock or debt, commercial banks were limited in what services they could offer.

The issuance capability was the province of the *investment* banks, which had to be independent institutions. In addition, it was left to individual states to determine the branching possibilities for banks within the state, and banks were barred from doing retail business across state lines. As a result, the U.S. banking system was a mixture of overlapping state and federal laws.

This was all changed by the mid-1990's, and since then we have seen strong expansion by many banks as they branch out in services and geographic scope. These developments mean that it is possible to do far more with a single bank—or bank holding company—than it was just a few years earlier.

For many larger and middle market companies, especially those with national retail business, the developing national banks can greatly simplify their banking networks, reducing the substantial bank service expenses these companies incurred before interstate banking was possible.

Another area—the elimination of much check float—has offered further opportunities for simplifying bank relations. Many banks have developed services to convert checks to electronic debits either at the point of sale (purchase) or in a lockbox that could be cleared through the automated clearing house (ACH) network. This accelerates the clearance of these checks and means that companies can use fewer banks for customer receipts. In addition, new federal legislation has legalized the use of electronic images to clear checks, eliminating the need to physically transport them back to the bank on which they were drawn.

With reduced check use, companies can simplify and consolidate their banking network needs. For banks it means that service charges for check processing will likely be decreasing as companies adopt more electronic methods. It remains to be seen whether this will cause increases in electronically handled transactions in the future.

Driving Forces

There are several driving forces behind corporate-banking relations, as shown in Figure 1-2. Some of them have decreased in intensity over time, or they have changed in the way that they affect bank relations. The need for credit facilities is discussed in Chapter 9.

Historical ties

The historical ties between an organization and its bank (or banks) may have originally been financial. For instance, as an organization grew, the bank that helped finance that growth was often rewarded with more business. Similarly, a bank that stayed with an organization in difficult times or came to its aid during a financial emergency was remembered in the good times. Conversely, banks that turned away from organizations in times of financial distress were not likely to receive a warm welcome later.

Figure 1-2: Driving Forces Behind Corporate-Bank Relations

Historical ties

Company service needs

Consultants

Geography

Need for credit facilities

Organizational pressures

Today this has changed—on both sides. Customers shift service providers periodically (e.g., with RFPs), and banks often decline to continue providing services to existing customers.

Large corporations consistently report they have been consolidating their bank relationships in recent years. Researchers, such as Phoenix-Hecht and Greenwich Associates, a Connecticut-based research firm, have all noted this trend. This means that how a bank provides services to a company is more important than ever. Treasury managers are not likely to look for a new bank to replace their current one unless they are dissatisfied with the service. As treasury managers rise in their organizations, they will naturally look for the banks with which they feel the most comfortable. Thus, non-financial management ties are important to maintain.

Company service needs

Another driving force is the nature of the company's service needs. The more customized or specialized they are, the more important the bank relationship is.

Many companies and governmental entities have some *plain vanilla* needs; i.e., their needs are satisfied by the standard bank service. However, companies in special industries (e.g., retail) may require customized banking services. For these companies, maintaining sound bank relationships usually outweighs price-shopping for the lowest cost services. Service cost is not ignored, of course; it is probably used to break ties. The banks that historically have provided services are likely to retain those accounts as long as the company's needs do not change, the company does not outgrow the bank, or the bank doesn't change via merger.

Consultants

Sometimes there are distinct, external factors that affect bank relationships. One such factor is the corporate treasury manager's experience with consultants. These consultants may be bankers or independent third parties. In either case, they play significant advisory roles in determining which institutions a corporation uses for bank non-credit services, or whether a service is needed at all by their recommendations and advice.

Consultants' recommendations may be affected by their own past experience, just as this affects a treasury manager's opinion of a financial institution. Consultants strive to be objective, but this can be difficult, especially if the consultant has had substantial negative experience with a bank (or banks).

Geography

Another driving force may be geography. Given the state of U.S. banking, it seems likely that we will see true nationwide branch banking in the near future. Consequently, treasury managers will not have to deal often with local banks even if they maintain decentralized operating locations.

Manufacturers used to need local banks near plants or sales offices, while retailers or fast food chains had to deal with hundreds or even thousands of local banks because of their widespread consumer locations. In fact, some states required local banking arrangements for payrolls (e.g., California and Florida), thus necessitating some local bank relationship management activities or the use of multiple drawee checks.

Today, it is possible to circumvent these barriers by using a combination of electronic services and the widespread branches of the largest banks. This has shifted the geographic driving force from the need to find numerous banks to service a wide area to find one or two banks that can service a wide geographic area.

Organizational pressures

Finally, organizational pressures can affect bank relationships. Mergers and acquisitions on both sides have had a major impact on bank relations. When two companies merge, there is usually considerable overlap between the two treasury groups. Bank consolidation and elimination is usually one result. The winners are likely to be determined by the strength of one of the driving forces mentioned above, i.e., which institution has provided the best services or was considered the major bank of the acquiring entity. The acquiring company usually doesn't throw out the other company's banking system without at least evaluating it. Also, the role of banks in the merger (e.g., support for or against an unfriendly takeover) may determine whether they will be considered for *any* future services at all.

When two banks merge, they also face questions of survival. It is possible that the acquired bank had a stronger relationship with a major customer than the acquiring bank did. Thus, if the "new" bank wants to retain that business, it must convince the major customer that nothing will change after the merger.

Parent-subsidiary relationships can also limit the options of a corporate treasury manager, especially at the subsidiary level. Corporate mandates about which banks to use may affect historical ties to other banks. The strength of centralized or decentralized treasury managers will be the deciding force in such cases.

Corporate philosophies toward centralization and/or decentralization change over time, so what exists today may be modified next year. However, many companies have recognized that at least for the time being there is a distinct benefit from centralizing. Obviously, this can have major impact on bank relations as well as on other corporate financial activities.

Ethical considerations

It is important to deal explicitly with some industry-specific ethical issues, and we have done so in the chapters that deal with the bank's point of view and the customer's point of view. Although the issues may be similar, the perspectives are often quite different.

In general, there has been a growing acceptance of a professional code of ethics, which has been a part of the professional certification program offered by the Association for Financial Professionals. To be sure, focus on a code of ethics is not something that is widely reported or discussed, unless there has been a recent industry "event" that has caused tremors throughout the corporate and banking world.

Chapter 1 ACTION ITEMS

§ Adopt an appropriate attitude with your banks, i.e., treat them as important service providers. Assure that this attitude change is understood and accepted by all staff members.

§ Establish and maintain a record (e.g., using a spreadsheet program) of all bank visits by company employees to banks and by bankers to company sites. Record dates, reasons for visits, and any actions/results from the meeting.

§ Establish and record an "open item" list of legislative and regulatory issues or events to track their status. Consider using the update or monitoring services of major trade associations, such as AFP or NACM.

Chapter 1 ACTION ITEMS (cont.)

§ List and describe any special services provided by your bank(s). Include all bank-supplied documentation. Note for each such service how long the bank has supplied the service and how you would have to handle the service if the bank stopped providing it.

§ If you use more than one bank for services, describe what each bank provides in general terms (e.g., Bank X provides cash management services that it was awarded after last RFP project.).

§ Establish a bank service charge monitoring spreadsheet model, tracking total service charges and bank fees paid (after any balance offset) monthly. Note months when price changes took effect.

2

Commodity or Value-Added?

How do you look at basic cash management services? Are they services you believe any number of banks–large and small– can provide to your satisfaction? Or do you think that there are only a few banks, perhaps just one, that can provide the services you need?

If you agree with the former opinion, you belong to the "commodity" thinkers. If you fall in the latter category, you see some value added by the bank(s). It is important to make this distinction because it can affect how you handle bank relations.

If you consider most bank services to be value-added services, you will be more likely to deal with a small number of banks and not always be shopping around for the best price. On the other hand, if you consider basic cash management services as commodities, you probably will be willing to switch banks regularly to keep the fees for these services as low as possible, although for more advanced or customized services, you may not be as price-sensitive.

Types of services

Most banks today can offer a full range of financial services, similar to those shown in Figure 2-1. Some of the services, such as netting and reinvoicing, are targeted for large, multinational firms, but most of the other services are appropriate for organizations of all sizes. In addition, some banks offer other specialized services, such as consulting and foreign exchange advisory services or multinational credit facilities.

You can use Figure 2-1 as a checklist when you are attempting to document current and potential bank services. I'll discuss each type of service shown in the figure in the sections that follow except for credit services, which I discuss in Chapter 8.

Cash Management Services

In the past, many banks believed that securing the corporate-bank relationship was determined primarily by satisfying a company's credit needs. Cash management services were regarded as subordinate to the credit services provided to the corporation. During the late 1970's and through the 1980's, banks were forced to rethink how they charged for cash management services as profits on credit services steadily decreased. In addition, as banks were able to measure profit performance for individual types of service groups, they began to recognize that non-credit services could provide them with the highest return on investment.

This rethinking changed to a marked shift in focus in the 1990's and into the 21st century as diminished spreads on loans and steady, low interest rates forced banks to develop alternate revenue streams. The expansion of the cash management services market helped banks replace the lost revenue from credit-based and money market services with fee-based income from non-credit services.

Many of the cash management services shown in Figure 2-1, such as lockbox, have been available for decades but have been modified to take advantage of modern technology and better means of communication. The newer services are the electronic ones, which can provide improved efficiencies in payment processing for bank customers of all sizes.

Lockboxes

Lockbox services are the oldest cash management service offered by banks to corporations and come in several varieties. Most banks offer a standard *wholesale lockbox*, which handles moderate volumes of large-dollar checks. As long as checks are accepted for payment by customers, some type of intercept service, such as a lockbox service, will be necessary. Traditional lockbox service provides reduced float and faster availability on check payments than you get by receiving checks at an organization's offices.

As large, multi-state banks have emerged from the consolidation in the banking industry, they have been able to take advantage of their locations to offer lockbox network services, which provide several lockbox collection points all tied to one central account within the same banking system or holding company. This type of service can be used to reduce mail float from payments as well as to concentrate funds without creating additional banking relations.

Another type of lockbox service is the *retail lockbox*, which is characterized by a high volume of small dollar checks from consumers (or retail customers). Typically, retail lockbox remittances are uniform, with a standard turnaround remittance document, a return envelope provided to the customer by the seller, and a simple payment transaction—a single check to pay a set amount. Most of the retail remittance documents are machine readable using optical character recognition (OCR) or other similar technologies. Retail lockbox services are not offered by all major banks because of the substantial investment in equipment, etc. that is required. However, many of the largest banks do offer this type of service for their customers, either in-house or through a referral to an outside, non-bank processor.

Recent technological improvements, especially one called *image processing*, have improved the quality and accuracy of lockbox services. These technologies have also allowed banks to link paper and electronic media. As most large and many medium-sized corporations use more than one bank for lockbox services, these services are usually tied in to the corporation's concentration network. This entails daily deposit reporting by the lockbox bank and concentration of funds by the corporation's main concentration bank.

Figure 2-1: Bank Services

Type of Service	Examples
Credit services	*Lines of credit, revolving credit agreements, letters of credit (standby type), bankers acceptances, medium-term loans (term loans)*
Cash management services	*Lockbox, controlled disbursements, zero balance accounts, account reconciliation, positive pay, wire transfers (of funds), ACH services, electronic data interchange (EDI) payments*
Information services	*Balance and transaction (detail) reporting, customer credit information (bank balances, loans outstanding, credit available), detailed account analyses, informal information: rates, transactions, treasury work station support (transaction detail)*
International/trade services	*Foreign exchange (FX) transaction services, international payments, letter of credit (commercial type) processing, documentary collections, overseas borrowing/financing (in-country, regional, and cross-border), netting and reinvoicing systems, advisory services, overseas cash management services*

(continued)

Figure 2-1: Bank Services (cont.)

Type of Service	*Examples*
Money market and investment services	*Investments and investment management (as broker-dealer), sweep investment services, custody and safekeeping services*
Card services	*Merchant card processing (debit and credit cards), purchasing cards, employee travel and entertainment (T&E) cards, employee pay cards*
Personal banking services	*Checking accounts for employees, mortgages, on-site banking/cashiering/ATM services, personal loans (e.g., to officers, company VIPs), trust (personal) services*
Other services	*Investment banking services, fiduciary services*

Disbursement services

Disbursement services can be regular corporate disbursements for payables or payroll through a standard checking account known as a *demand deposit account,* (DDA), a *zero balance account* (ZBA), or a *controlled disbursement account.* ZBA services allow corporations to operate many accounts (e.g., disbursement, deposit, and payroll) at the same bank without worrying about funding each account separately. The ZBAs are all tied to a master account that gets funded daily.

Controlled disbursement services are usually priced higher than regular disbursements, but they offer same-day notification of check clearings. This allows a corporate treasury manager to transfer the exact amount of funds into the disbursement account on the same day the checks clear, thus eliminating the guesswork that might otherwise be necessary.

Controlled disbursement accounts may also be set up as ZBAs, especially when a company has multiple controlled disbursement accounts and wishes to consolidate the funding into one master account. Otherwise, combining a ZBA and controlled disbursement account would be unnecessary and would only add more service charges.

Reconciliation

Closely linked to disbursement accounts are reconciliation services. Banks offer a wide variety of these services, ranging from *partial reconciliation,* in which the bank sends a tape of the checks paid for the accounting period (typically a month), to *full reconciliation,* in which the corporation provides a tape of checks issued and voided and the bank reconciles paid items and shows a list of outstanding items at the end of the accounting period. Most banks today that have converted to image processing of checks deposited with the bank can also send their customers a CD-ROM containing check images (front and back) of all checks paid during the monthly period. A CD-ROM is a convenient tool that can make researching vendor payment inquiries much easier than was previously possible.

Another service usually grouped with the reconciliation family is *positive pay services.* Positive pay services help protect disbursement accounts against check fraud. You provide your bank with a file of all checks issued, and it verifies that clearing checks are on the file and have not been altered. The bank compares check number and amount and notifies you of any discrepancy. It allows you a predetermined short period of time to resolve the discrepancy and tell the bank what to do about it. Some banks are beginning to add payee name and transmission of an image of all checks that do not agree with the issue file as part of the verification process.

Wire transfers

A widely used cash management service is *wire transfer.* Many organizations use wire transfer services when they have to move funds on the same day, such as to move funds to other banks or to broker-dealers as part of an investment transaction.

This usually means using Fedwire, the Federal Reserve's wire transfer system. Corporations can access Fedwire only through banks, and they do so through a computer terminal, personal computer, or via telephone. The more automated and repetitive these transfers are, the less the banks charge for the service.

ACH services

In addition to wire transfer services, most organizations use *automated clearing house* (ACH) services offered by banks. ACH transactions can be debits (withdrawals) or credits (deposits). Unlike Fedwire, the ACH cannot move funds from one bank to another bank on the same day. There is a minimum of one day's delay. Some banks offer what they call "same-day ACH," but this is restricted to ACH-type transactions among entities within the same banking system or bank holding company. ACH transactions include such high-growth transactions as direct deposit of payroll, pension fund and retirement fund payouts, and dividend disbursements. The ACH is also used heavily for funds concentration, having replaced paper-based depository transfer checks and other methods.

Corporations also have access (through banks) to two international settlement or communications systems. These are the Clearing House Interbank Payment System (CHIPS), which is operated by the New York Clearing House Association and is used to settle most of the international interbank dollar transactions, and the Society for Worldwide Interbank Financial Telecommunications (S.W.I.F.T.), which is an international message switching system now operating in some 68 countries.

EDI services

Financial *electronic data interchange* (EDI) services are related to wire transfer and ACH services. These include receiving and transmitting corporate-to-corporate trade payments, translating among various EDI formats and assisting corporations in converting trading partners to the electronic environment. Some banks offering financial EDI are also able to combine electronic receipts with paper receipts through their lockbox services and transmit the consolidated information to the corporation for more efficient accounts receivable posting.

Information Services

Closely aligned with cash management services are information services. Banks can provide a wealth of information about your banking activity, but information reporting is not inexpensive. You need to think carefully about how much information you really need vs. the costs of obtaining it. For instance, many banks will store your daily information reports for extended periods of time, basically for as long as you wish. You have to decide how long you really need to retain it – especially if you are retaining your own copy of the same data.

I think that many companies overpay for information storage without realizing the true costs involved. This is something to scrutinize carefully on your account analysis statements. Information services charges have shown steady growth as part of bank service revenues in recent years.

Balance and transaction reporting

The information service that is tied most closely with cash management services is *information reporting*. Information reporting services include reports showing bank account balances and itemized lists of detailed transactions. These reports are accessed via your PC and are generally available at the start of the work day and continually throughout the remainder of the day. The services also permit funds transfers to be initiated from a personal computer. Although most information services only report information from a single bank, most of them have the capability to offer consolidated balance reporting from other banks in the organization's network.

Information about bank balance levels and transaction reconcilement are vital to effective corporate cash management. Treasury managers compute the cash position of their company daily, and one of the principal inputs to the position is the net bank position. This is reported through bank information reporting services. Consequently, organizations use the information reporting services of their major banks because these banks handle most of the organization's cash management transactions.

Some companies also ask their banks for transaction information that does not appear on the daily reports. A good example of this is a request for the lockbox department to call, fax, or e-mail the names and amounts of items received in lockbox for the current day. This can become an expensive way to get information because it involves lockbox staff. Any time you ask your bank to do something that requires substantial human intervention, you can expect to pay a higher price than if the information can be captured and sent to you in a more automated fashion. Fortunately, the application of imaging technology in bank lockbox services can make this conversion. Both you and your bank gain with imaging – you get your information in an electronic file, and the bank does not have to dedicate anyone to notify you.

Most treasury managers in larger organizations use specialized software to obtain bank information services. Used in this manner–to download balance and other bank information into a data base on a local PC, to make funds transfers, and to manage the daily cash position–the PCs are usually referred to as *treasury work stations.*

Not too long ago, many banks offered treasury work station products to larger customers. However, most banks abandoned treasury work stations as a product line, at least in the U.S. I believe that banks realized that they were not going to be able to offer a profitable software-based product line. Banks have been content to supply information to treasury work stations (for a fee), rather than creating and maintaining the software.

Other types of information

Banks provide another type of bank account information to their corporate customers in the form of monthly *account analysis* statements. The vast majority of banks provide account analysis statements in paper form, although a few have begun to provide the statements electronically. These statements are the building blocks of bank compensation and will be discussed in more detail in Chapter 4.

Banks are also good sources for *trade credit* information. Many banks offer credit reviews of corporations to other corporations considering extending those firms trade credit. This may be effective for small volumes, but it can be expensive or inefficient for larger numbers of customers, in which case use of a third party service provider (e.g., Dun & Bradstreet) may be more cost effective.

In addition, banks provide many types of other information that treasury managers require from time to time. For example, many banks report their foreign exchange rates to corporate customers via the customers' PCs. They also provide money market rates this way. Banks are often storehouses of historical information on interest rates or other rates that corporations may need.

International/Trade Services

Major multinational banks offer a full menu of international services, such as those shown previously in this chapter (Figure 2-1). However, many domestic banks do not offer a full array of international services. Organizations with moderate international business look to their U.S. main bank (or banks) for these services. As organizations grow globally, they may look to major foreign banks and major U.S. multinational banks (although these ranks may be thinning) for assistance.

As you get involved with overseas operations, major multinational banks become useful service providers as well as information sources on issues and events in foreign markets. You should maintain relations with one or more multinational banks if you want to have an effective treasury system worldwide. Many of these banks have local operations that are full-service banks in foreign markets, so you can use their branches as local banks and as cross-border funds movers.

Major foreign and multinational banks generally offer advisory services that can be helpful to U.S. corporations setting up operations overseas. These services are frequently offered on a consulting basis (for a fee), but some banks offer advisory services to their major customers at no cost or for a nominal subscription charge.

FX transactions and advisory services are not offered for free by the major banks; these are good profit-makers for them. Banks charge a commission on FX trades or realize a profit from a favorable buy-sell spread. They offer advisory services for an annual fee. Other international services, such as netting, reinvoicing, payments, borrowings, financings, and cash management services, also generate fee income for the banks offering them.

Money Market and Investment Services

This has been an active area for many banks. The repeal of the Glass-Steagall Act has allowed banks to become active players in more financial markets and can offer a full menu of money market investments, money management, and other services. Often, an organization will start with a simple service, such as an overnight investment sweep account.

Sweep investment services

With bank *sweep arrangements*, an organization can arrange for its banks to "sweep" excess balances over a minimum level into a short-term investment account (with the bank) or into a separate portfolio, which can be managed by internal staff or an outside party (such as the bank or another financial institution). The customer is notified daily of the amount invested without making an investment decision.

This service has been marketed heavily to smaller and middle market companies. Overnight sweeps essentially are mechanisms for corporations to earn interest on their checking account (DDA) balances. In times of significantly low interest rates, many organizations turn to sweep accounts because investment transactions can be made daily for a flat monthly fee, whereas investing in individual securities would entail additional charges, such as funds transfers and custody fees.

Investment managers

When the amount invested in a sweep account passes a threshold (e.g., $5 million invested), there is enough to consider making direct investments or using the bank's money management services to invest the excess funds for a fee. In such cases the funds are transferred to the money manager daily, and the manager invests them within guidelines established at the outset of the relationship and adjusted on an ongoing basis.

Custody and safekeeping

Banks also offer *custody* and *safekeeping* services, which entail recording and holding securities in the organization's investment portfolio(s). Since most investment transactions today are paperless, custody services have been simplified, and it has been easier to consolidate all custody services to one bank's system. Many banks also offer custody reports, such as maturity schedules or investment portfolio details, to customers via bank information reporting services.

Card Services

Banks can offer an array of card services. *Merchant card processing services* help you accept debit and credit cards. Most banks offer both MasterCard and Visa processing services, with electronic clearing of the transactions and ACH deposit of sales proceeds on a routine basis. There may be differences in rates and transaction charges among banks, so it pays to shop around for these services. You can look at them as commodity services since the processing is fairly straightforward, and your net proceeds from the card transactions can be electronically deposited in any bank.

Purchasing cards

In addition, card services can include *purchasing cards* (p-cards), which allow you to consolidate small expense items and pay them in one (electronic) payment monthly. If used properly – i.e., for small purchases of supplies, equipment, etc., p-card services can be efficient tools. They allow you to eliminate issuing many small checks and to control the suppliers used and the amounts spent. Note that with p-cards, you decide to whom you will issue them, and for this reason, you hold the liability for their misuse (unlike with credit cards discussed below).

As was the case with merchant card processing, p-cards can be treated as commodity-type services. However, some banks offer combined T&E and purchasing card services, and you may find this more attractive than just obtaining the lowest price.

Other employee cards

Banks offer *employee credit cards* for T&E expenses. With this service, your employees are responsible for the purchases, and the bank reviews and approves each employee you wish to have a card. If you include your T&E card service needs as part of a larger service selection decision, such as when you use RFPs for a bundle of services, you may be able to obtain lower prices on the cards.

Banks also offer *pay card services*, which function like debit cards and are used to pay employees who do not have bank accounts. State, local, and federal governmental entities have used these cards to distribute financial aid to low-income recipients for years, and they have proven to be effective tools. You should consider using them if you have significant numbers of part-time or temporary employees, as well as for those employees without bank accounts.

Personal Banking Services

Another aspect of bank relations is the personal banking side. This can range from arranging loans and mortgages to referring executives to outside financial planners and advisors.

Because of the confidential nature of most of these transactions, corporations usually look to their main bank relationships for help with these services. They are often delicate matters to handle.

Other Services

In addition to the services already discussed, other services include specialized fiduciary services, such as stock registrar, bond trustee, long-term debt/equity underwriting, commercial paper (sales), and processing of stock tender offers (depositary services for mergers). A company may turn to its main banks for these services, many of which may be one-time events or may be needed at infrequent times.

Since there is often ample lead time in arranging these services, establishing them should not pose major problems. Some of these services may be offered by a subsidiary of the bank holding company.

Banks also offer investment banking services. These include long-term debt and equity underwriting, advisory services on financial structure, and merger and acquisition assistance.

Chapter 2 ACTION ITEMS

§ Using Figure 2-1 as a guide, establish an "inventory" of bank services, using a spreadsheet program. For each service note the following:
  - Organizational units using service—enter "N/A" for services that are not used
  - Total monthly service charges—for cash management services, post from monthly bank account analysis statements (note that some banks provide charges by groupings, which should conform to Figure 2-1); for other services, post from bank invoices/charges
  - Date when service was last awarded and what procedure, such as request for proposal (RFP), was used

§ Develop a list of unused services from the inventory described above. Categorize each unused service as to potential use, such as high, moderate, and low, using a scale of 1-3 or 1- 5. For each of the highest-priority items, add descriptions of how well one or more of your current banks could provide the service. You can even add a "most likely provider" for each higher-rated service.

§ If you use one or more banks for foreign exchange (FX) services, such as trading in spot and forward contracts, establish and maintain transaction records, showing bank, contact name, currency or currencies traded, transaction dates, transaction amounts in foreign currency and U.S. dollars, and any other comments on the transactions.

Chapter 2 ACTION ITEMS (cont.)

§ For money market services, such as sweep investment accounts, track the amounts invested, interest income, expenses involved (e.g., cost of sweep service). Do the same kind of tracking if money managers are used.

§ For card services, record and update, as necessary, the provider of the card service, charges for the service, how recently the card business was awarded and how this was done, and any comments on how well/poor card service has been.

3

Thinking Like a Banker

In considering how to manage your bank relationships, it is important to understand how banks look at relationships. Banks are profit-making (or profit-seeking) institutions; they are not in business to lose money. Bank profits come from the loans they make, from returns on other investments, from spreads on financial transactions (e.g., foreign exchange) and from fees (or the equivalent in balances) from non-credit services, such as cash management. More progressive banks look at the total relationship with their customers, and that means that you should be aware of everything your organization does with your bank (or banks, if there is more than one).

I do not mean to imply that all bankers see their relationships this way, but the good ones do. In the past, banks could count on steady income from spreads on loans and other financial products. However, in times of low interest rates, they found these products were no longer providing adequate returns. As a result, banks placed more emphasis on fee-based income, which meant that cash management and other similar services were counted on to pick up the revenue slack. Banks also found that fee-based services, which include cash management services, offer a far greater return to the bank than loans or other transactions.

As a result, bankers have changed their approach in many cases, now requiring some level of fee-based services for providing short-term credit facilities (e.g., a line of credit). This switch can create problems for you if you want to keep your cash management business concentrated in one bank but need more than one bank for your credit needs. In such cases, you may have to split up your business to get what you want. You may be able to split up your business so that one bank still remains your main bank, while the other bank (or banks) receives a narrow group of services, such as local or lockbox deposit services.

Profitability Items

As we might expect, typical returns for different types of bank services vary widely. These differences have become evident to banks as they evaluate individual product lines and attempt to tap into those services that have higher revenue and profitability potential. While the returns may be higher for many fee-based types of services, it is important to keep in mind the scale of the returns. By far the largest amount of revenue should come from loans, while the returns from the other types are higher relatively but smaller in absolute terms.

Fee-based services, such as cash management services, foreign exchange, and swaps transactions can provide the greatest rate of return. The return on loans depends on the type of borrower. For example, banks can obtain a higher rate of return from smaller companies (i.e., middle market) than from large company borrowings. This is due to the competitive nature of these loans—large companies have other competitive alternatives like commercial paper, while smaller companies have far less choice. Competitive shopping by larger borrowers may reduce the customer loyalty banks show to them compared to how they treat smaller borrowers. This is shown in the Phoenix-Hecht Blue Book of Bank Prices for 2002-2003 report, which found that almost 40% of large corporations reported that they had credit commitments reduced by their banks, while only 15% of smaller companies did.

This helps explain why so many banks have been concentrating their calling efforts on the middle market segment. Banks have changed the way they look at customer profitability just as organizations have tightened their levels of compensation and the amount of services purchased. Banks are no longer willing to settle for providing limited services that do not provide the rate of return they seek.

Bank costs

This raises the question of whether banks know their costs for individual services. In the past, banks did not consider it vital to know their costs precisely, so they did not spend much time trying to track costs and revenues by product line. In today's environment, however, they can no longer afford to offer a wide menu of services without some idea of what the services cost.

Many banker friends of mine still hold that banks do not have a good handle on their costs, preferring instead to look at revenues and costs at a more aggregated level. I believe many banks still take this approach, but I believe that others have taken a more detailed look at their product lines and have stopped offering services that do not offer sufficient returns. For instance, I believe this is the reason that some banks have reduced the types and locations of their lockbox services or have sought customer guarantees on transaction volumes before upgrading a service line by investing in newer technologies.

Bank revenues

Breaking down cash management revenue, as E&Y does in its 2003 survey, shows how much revenue banks derive from various services:

- Basic checking account (DDA) services   40.0%
- Wire transfer services   12.5%
- Check clearing services   11.5%
- Wholesale lockbox services   9.5%
- Information reporting services   9.0%
- ACH/EDI services   6.0%
- Controlled disbursement services   4.0%
- Account reconciliation services   4.0%
- Retail lockbox services   3.5%

Revenues from DDA, check clearing, and retail lockbox services decreased slightly from the previous year. The other services all grew with the exception of controlled disbursement services, which remained the same as the previous years. ACH/EDI and information reporting services showed the strongest growth, reporting 11% and 10% growth rates over previous year levels.

The Effects of Competition

Although banks can make substantial returns from non-credit services, the market for these services is intensely competitive. As bank consolidation continues, however, the amount of competition for corporate business will probably decrease. Already, many companies have found that they have fewer choices for service and, therefore, have less bargaining power than in previous times. This means that you will not realize significant price differences among banks when bidding out your business.

Bank staffing

Understand that this has become a big business and that banks have dedicated substantial amounts of resources to establish their market shares. A good indication of the resources involved is the number of people active in cash management sales and service. According to the 2003 E&Y study, the largest banks averaged around 550 employees in sales, product development and management, customer services, and other support. In fact, the five largest banks had almost three times that number involved. Mid-sized banks average 100 employees, while smaller banks average 30. These are impressive numbers.

Note that these numbers include customer service, product management, and sales functions. As we might expect, staff size varies by bank size, with the largest banks showing more than half their employees in customer service roles, while the smallest banks only have almost half their employees in customer service roles. The largest banks have almost 30% of their cash management staff devoted to sales, while the smallest banks have almost half of their staffs in sales.

Unbundling charges

When individual service profitability was not as important to banks, they tended to bundle the charges for individual cash management services. Price differentials for large volume or for extreme customization were common, but the degree of current unbundling of service charges today is of a different order of magnitude. For example, many banks used to charge for most of their processing through a few components.

Today, there may be two or three times the charge components for the same service. Unbundling in this way allows banks to charge for various portions of a complete service or to charge more to those customers that require additional bank resources. This unbundling is now common for most bank non-credit services.

As banks identify their operating costs and relate them to individual services, they may find that their "optimal" price is not competitive. This has caused substantial price increases in recent years, as mentioned in Chapter 1. Figure 3-1 shows the services that had the largest price increases reported in the 2002-2003 *Phoenix-Hecht Blue Book of Bank Prices.*

The frequency of price discounting is far less than one would expect. Also, the frequency of general price increases is not that common. Banks tend to increase prices for non-credit services moderately, usually every two years or so unless changes in the services justify a change sooner.

New services

For many banks, it doesn't pay to be a pioneer in developing new services. This may be because of the similarity among services from bank to bank. It also reflects the reluctance of customers to switch bank relationships to the first bank to offer a particular service. Customers typically take note of new services and then ask their bank when it will be offering that service.

There has been, however, a slight departure from this general rule recently. Banks that have become very active in electronic data interchange (EDI) have experienced increases in other business, especially paper-based cash management business (e.g., lockbox).

Figure 3-1: Increases in Service Charge Pricing
(1999-2002)

Service	Avg. Price Increase	Avg. List Price (2002)
Reconciliation processing (partial)	22.2%	$0.05
International incoming wire	20.3%	$13.89
Outgoing wire (manual, repetitive)	19.8%	$15.15
Reporting–Term/Net (previous day)	18.1%	$0.18
Stop payment (manual)	17.5%	$24.34
Deposit reconciliation processing	17.1%	$0.10
Wholesale lockbox item processing	17.0%	$0.45
Reconciliation maintenance (partial)	16.0%	$63.95
ZBA maintenance (sub account)	15.9%	$26.00
Return item processing (regular)	15.7%	$5.55
Branch furnished coin (rolled)	15.7%	$0.12
Reporting–Term/Net (intraday)	15.2%	$0.24
General ACH manitenance	15.1%	$54.47
Outgoing wire (manual, free-form)	15.1%	$29.60

Defining the Relationship

For many banks, the opportunity to function as a corporation's *main* bank is important, and they work long and hard to achieve this status. A main bank is the one that a corporation may turn to first for new non-credit and credit business. It is also the one that the organization tends to rely on for technological updates or news on current issues. Banks seek main roles for a very obvious reason – it means more business for the bank and probably for an extended period of time because organizations do not change main banks frequently.

Figure 3-2 gives some examples of the non-credit and credit services typically provided by an organization's main bank. As

Figure 3-2: Role of a Main Bank

Cash management services
- Cash concentration
- Controlled disbursements (although this may be elsewhere)
- Funds transfer (for funding operating bank accounts)
- Balance reporting

Custody/safekeeping for the short-term investment portfolio

Issuance of commercial paper notes

Money market services

Credit services
- Agent for revolving credit agreements
- Largest short-term line of credit

Financial advisory services

Foreign exchange (possibly a major portion)

Letters of credit

the figure shows, when a bank serves as a main bank, it plays the major role with a customer. As such, it is often privy to business plans and other information that other banks will not know.

Obviously, all banks cannot be main banks to all their customers. How do banks act in minor roles? The best rule of thumb is to strive to provide the best possible service to the customer.

Customers do not constantly shift their cash management business. Thus, the banks that provide the most valued services are likely to be in the final bank "group." It seems advisable, then, that strong performance in a minor role can be worthwhile. Banks that accept a minor role but continue to call regularly with new ideas or input on issues will likely be included in future corporate plans. Banks that take on a minor role but never (or hardly ever) call on the customer are more likely to be dropped from future considerations.

Industry leaders

Many organizations only want to deal with industry leaders in service or, more recently, in financial performance and stability. Therefore, if a bank is not among the leaders, is it likely to get much business? The answer to this question is not a simple "no" because industry leaders don't stay that way forever. A concerted effort by a bank that historically has had operational or financial problems or a reputation for being "back in the pack" can turn things around.

Since most customers really judge a bank by the quality of the service it provides (and, to a slightly lesser degree, its price), no bank should consider itself "out of the market." Also, because most cash management services are not unique (i.e., most banks can provide the same, general level of service), the quality of the service is paramount. This can be improved quickly by better customer service and relatively modest investment by a bank, if it does not continue to have financial distress.

The "R" word

The "R" word used to mean relationship, but now means revenue for most banks. Even so, it pays for bankers and their customers to maintain some aspects of the traditional approach to establishing effective customer-bank relationships.

The calling effort is the key to a successful bank relationship, major or minor. This effort cannot be limited to the calling officer only; it should entail calls from many different areas of the bank. If technical cash management services are needed (e.g., involving systems applications), then the savvy calling officer will know to bring together the right people from the bank and customer side. As mentioned previously, banks have invested heavily in personnel to serve their customers properly, so you should expect to have knowledgeable bankers calling on you.

Bank calls

Good calls result from the banker and the treasury manager knowing and trusting each other. Bad calls are those without purpose or those with a heavy sales "pitch," often for a product that you already have and have no interest in changing. "Do your homework," is a sound motto for the bank calling officer, especially if the homework is done in advance. This applies equally to you if you want to get the most out of your bank meeting. Minimizing the wasted time on calls pays off for both sides, and both sides should be interested in making the most of meetings.

One other factor in a successful calling effort is stability. Banks that maintain the same calling group for an extended period of time are looked upon more favorably by their customers. It is very difficult for a bank to develop an effective working relationship with its customers if it has a reputation for shifting personnel too often.

The main bank relationship

The main relationship is fostered through hard work and a tradition of cooperation, commitment, and communication. Cooperation comes about through the ability of a organization's treasury staff to forge an effective working arrangement with the bank.

The commitment must come from both the organization and the bank to provide adequate resources *to each other*. It must be a two-way street; only then will both sides get from the relationship what they need to sustain it.

Finally, communication is paramount. Banks cannot guess what a customer needs. The treasury manager must tell his or her banker. Regular meetings with preplanned agendas can be effective. In any case, a periodic meeting to trade information and discuss company and bank developments is mandatory. For this reason alone, it helps if your main bank is based close by.

Note also that some very large companies have more than one main bank. Often, these companies have set up leads for major product lines or for major activities (e.g., financing, operations). However, there is some movement toward minimizing the number of banks an organization deals with, and this usually translates into just one major bank.

To a lesser extent, non-main relationships do not require the same level of commitment as main relationships. But, main bank shifts are not likely to be to a newcomer. Today's second-tier bank may be tomorrow's first-tier bank.

Why main bank relationships end

Losing a main relationship does not happen very often, nor does it happen overnight. Sometimes the loss is due to forces outside the bank's control, such as when the company is acquired by another with a different main bank. Merged companies tend to settle on one main bank, so unless the same bank is the main bank for both sides in a merger, one bank will lose out.

Likewise, mergers between banks may cause changes in main bank relationships. Here again, it can depend on the banks involved, but a customer may decide that the new merged bank is not what it wants as a main bank, perhaps because of a less-than-satisfactory relationship with the acquiring bank.

A bank may also voluntarily give up a main relationship if it is facing operational or financial difficulties. It may also give up a relationship if it decides that the company or the company's industry does not fit the profile of desired customers.

Risks in credit and non-credit services

Banks make decisions about credit services continually. They look for a customer's ability to repay on a timely basis and for possible collateral. They also consider economic influences and the stability of the customer's main lines of business.

While you may know about risks in credit services, you may not be fully aware of the risks to your banks with non-credit services. Banks must make provisional credit to customers for non-credit services. This occurs in such services as wire transfers, lockbox and check collections, controlled disbursements, cash concentration, and foreign exchange. For instance, in the case of a wire transfer, the bank must assure itself that its customer has the funds in its account before completing the transfer. If the customer does not have sufficient funds, the bank may still make the transfer, based on its belief (and experience) that the customer will have the necessary funds in its account before the close of business.

This same rationale holds true for other cash management products, such as controlled disbursements. In this case, for example, the bank must be certain that the customer will be able to fund its account properly if it does not maintain its concentration account with that bank. For deposits, the bank may want to be certain that the customer is keeping sufficient minimum balances to cover the overall float in the account or to cover the amount of daily returned items (if significant).

Wire transfers and ACH

There is very little risk in same-day, wire-funded receipts because a wire transfer is an irrevocable transfer of funds. On the other hand, ACH credits involve considerable risk for a bank.

Banks generally like to generate direct deposit of payroll one or two days before the effective date. This means that if a bank generates the payroll on Monday for a Wednesday payday, the transfers are effective on Wednesday. The company funds the payroll on Wednesday, the employees get paid on Wednesday, and if there's no problem, then all is settled on Wednesday. However, the rules of the ACH say that as soon as the bank initiates the transactions and puts them into the ACH (that is, Monday), the bank is on the hook for that money, regardless of what happens in the interim.

Theoretically, the bank could try to get the money back, but are the employees likely to give up their paychecks? The receiving bank really has no liability. So, the originating bank is taking two days' credit risk on behalf of its customer when it initiates any kind of ACH credit, including direct deposit of payroll.

CHIPS

There is some risk in payments made through the Clearing House Interbank Payment System (CHIPS). The CHIPS system offers same-day transfers of funds (same-day value) subject to end-of-day settlement. It differs from Fedwire, which has immediate settlement and irrevocable transfers. Banks in the CHIPS system build up net credit or debit positions with each other throughout the day. The bank that is sent more credits than it sends out is at risk, because the other bank may not be able to settle at the end of the day.

If the bank facing the risk has allowed the customer to take out the money, assuming that all the transactions will settle at the end of the day, then the bank is subject to the loss of those funds. CHIPS rules call for unwinding all transactions in the CHIPS system if one of the players cannot settle. Then the whole system is settled without that player. If you have a net credit position with that player, you'll lose some money if you let the beneficiary of those transfers take out the money or use it for some purpose before the next day.

Overdrafts

It is one thing to make a credit decision, but it's another to have the information and establish the procedures to monitor daylight overdrafts on an intraday basis. Banks must be able to monitor overdrafts immediately from the start of business and need consolidated positions. They will have to develop sophisticated systems so that responsible people are the ones authorizing these credit exposures. Clerks in the wire transfer room and in the lockbox department are not the people who should be making decisions about extending credit to companies.

Banks also face risks in such areas as foreign exchange trading since FX contracts are not funded until later dates (e.g., one or two days for spot contracts and longer for forward contracts), so your bank has to be sure that you will be able to pay when it is time to do so.

Longer-term risks

For the most part, banks do not face long-term risks when offering non-credit services or making corporate loans. There are occasions when banks do have to consider longer-term risks, such as when they offer medium-term (2-10 years) term loans or arrange for private placements of debt or for bond issues. These risks will be reflected in the loan covenants that the bank will

Figure 3-3: Typical Loan Covenants

Affirmative (or positive) covenants require:
- Maintaining minimum levels of property and casualty insurance
- Timeliness of loan and interest payments (debt service, in general)
- Timeliness of other fundamental corporate obligations (e.g., taxes)
- General soundness of the company's business, including the maintenance of minimum or specified levels of:

    Working capital ratios
    Profitability ratios
    Interest coverage ratios
    Specified levels of profitability
    Financial reports on a regular basis

Restrictive (or negative) covenants prohibit certain activities, such as:
- Defaulting on (any) loan
- Sale/transfer of tangible assets of the company
- General actions that would decrease the value of collateralized assets or would prevent the lender from collecting the loan
- Taking on any (more) senior debt without prior approval
- Additional corporate acquisitions (without approval)
- Acquisition of other corporate equity positions
- Long-term investing
- Restrictions on dividend payouts
- Corporate guarantees of other debt, etc. (e.g., for a subsidiary or joint venture)

(continued)

Figure 3-3: Typical Loan Covenants (cont.)

Cross default:
- The failure to pay back any loan (or interest) automatically triggers defaults in other loans

Lender protection covenants:
- Capital adequacy costs— allows the lender to pass along any (and all) costs associated with central bank capital adequacy requirements
- Hold harmless clauses for acts of God, economic emergencies, etc.

---

seek. Typical loan covenants are listed in Figure 3-3. The extent of the covenants depends on the financial strength of the borrower at the time of the transaction and over the life of the debt.

Loan covenants fall into three categories: affirmative or positive, restrictive or negative and lender protection. Lenders tighten the covenants based on their assessment of the corporation's creditworthiness. These covenants are negotiable to a great degree. This is where it is extremely valuable to have developed a strong main bank relationship. A company's main bank is usually a good source for realistic covenant restrictions in any loan, so if a corporation is likely to require considerable bank borrowing, maintaining strong bank relationships is a must.

Intangibles and Ethics

When opening a new location, a company may find that it needs a local bank for intangible services—such as personal banking services for employees—for a short period of time. This is especially true if the new location is far removed from the corporation's main bank. In the past, many organizations did not deal specifically with this issue, simply assuming that there would be enough interest on the local bank's part in establishing new business. Other organizations established a special program at a local level, with specific, mutually agreed upon levels of support from the local bank and specific levels of compensation.

It is in the corporation's best interest to deal with such intangible services explicitly. Otherwise, neither the bank nor other corporate personnel understand what services are being provided and how they are being compensated for. Because intangible services can often be nebulous, it is important for customer-bank relations that they be made as tangible, or identified, as possible. In this way, the treasury manager can maintain good relationships with the company's banks and with internal corporate contacts.

Ethical considerations

Two techniques that some banks use—low-balling and bait-and-switch—can damage a customer relationship irreparably. Also, some banks may attempt a new type of bait-and-switch, offering an expensive form of the service with the intention of selling a lower-priced one all the while. These techniques can destroy the trust on which customer-bank relationships must depend.

Most experienced treasury managers will not automatically take the lowest price in a competitive situation. Furthermore, just as bankers talk to each other, so do treasury managers. Banks that have used these techniques will quickly get labeled accordingly.

Another questionable activity is the so-called impartial "free" consulting project. Some treasury managers seek banks that will conduct consulting studies (e.g., lockbox studies) for free. Many experienced treasury managers avoid this, however, because they have found that the results may be far from impartial.

Although it occurs very infrequently, some banks are sometimes thought to stack the model inputs to favor their own availability schedules, for example. They do this by excluding specific availabilities from other banks while supplying their own or by using city averages for mail times for other collection points but their own actual averages. The old adage, "You get what you pay for," is most appropriate here. Banks that do this should also consider whether it is truly worthwhile.

Board links—both ways, bank to customer and vice versa—can create artificial situations and possible hidden or perceived attitudes toward the other side. For instance, a treasury manager may be reluctant to bring up problems with a bank because a senior company executive sits on the bank's board and is thought to be protective of the bank (translated, this means: does not want to hear bad news). Another example is when the bank attempts to use the board presence to garner new business. This can create animosity toward the bank from the treasury manager and can erode the relationship in the long run. Banks using this technique should consider the longer-term ramifications of their actions.

Other board memberships by senior executives may be less visible, such as membership by an executive on a local bank board. As long as these links do not create conflicts at the local level, they may not be dangerous to the overall company. The possibility of such links should be dealt with directly in the company's bank policy to avoid any misunderstandings.

Chapter 3 ACTION ITEMS

§ Set up a spreadsheet model to track service charges. Use Figure 3-1 as a guide for the model, or subscribe to the Phoenix-Hecht *Blue Book of Bank Prices*.

- Compare, as much as possible, your individual service charge items with those shown in Figure 3-1 or in the *Blue Book*.
- Monitor the differences, if any, over time, researching those items that exceed your tolerance level (e.g., +/- 10%).

§ Using Figure 3-2 as a checklist, fill in the items shown for your current main or primary bank. Research any services you cannot document to be sure that the services, if applicable to your situation, are being provided satisfactorily.

Chapter 3 ACTION ITEMS (cont.)

§ Evaluate each of your banks as to acquisition potential. Use past experience and other trade reports as guides. Formulate your "reaction" plan if any of your banks were to be acquired or were to be involved in a substantial acquisition.

§ Establish a bank overdraft report, recording each instance of an overdraft in a spreadsheet program. For each overdraft situation, record the following data items:
  - Date of overdraft
  - Account involved
  - Organizational unit involved
  - Reason for overdraft – flag any overdrafts caused by bank error to be checked vs. the bank account analysis statement (it should not appear on the statement).
  - Amount of overdraft
  - Charge for overdraft (check against analysis statement)

§ Maintain a current list of all medium-term and long-term debt covenants, using Figure 3-4 as a guide. Flag especially onerous covenants to be eliminated or softened during the next negotiation session.

4

Compensation—Get It Right!

The least understood and most neglected aspect of managing bank relations is compensation. Yet bank compensation clearly is one of the most important considerations in your relationship with your bank.

In this chapter I discuss the forms of bank compensation and which approach is more feasible. I will review the primary form of compensation documentation—the bank account analysis statement. I also discuss the process of bank selection and why corporations make changes to their group of banks.

Underlying assumptions

Historically, banks have been flexible about compensation levels, but not about methods; compensating balances were the main method. In recent years, this has changed substantially. Today, customers are more likely to compensate their banks with fees than with collected balances. In fact, most customers actually use a combination of the two.

I will assume that you look like the typical organization and compensate your bank(s) monthly by a combination method—receiving an offset for the value of your balances against the total bank charges and paying the remainder by fee. In the rare instances that your balances translate into a value that is higher than your total service charges, you should negotiate with your banks to carry over excess balance values for the next month or two. This carry-over should be negotiated before-hand, however. It is unrealistic to expect the bank to agree to such an arrangement on the spot.

Choosing the Best Compensation Method

In the past, when interest rates were low and did not change much from year to year, senior executives and industry analysts regarded cash in the organization's bank accounts as a good sign of liquidity and a convenient means of bank compensation. However, as interest rates became more volatile and increased substantially, this view changed. Cash could be put to work to become an earning asset, and it was not good to have it sit idly in the bank.

As a result, organizations have switched from using compensating balances exclusively. At first, treasury managers attempted to make a complete switch from balances to fees, but they soon recognized that this was often impossible to manage.

Fee compensation

Compensation by fee is usually less expensive because of two main factors:

- Banks assign value to average compensating balances through an earnings credit that is typically less than a comparable short-term corporate rate. This is because the general credit rate is based on a short-term money market rate, usually the 90-day U.S. Treasury bill rate. Most investors can beat this rate.

- The earnings credit rate is reduced by the reserve requirement banks are assessed by the Federal Reserve, currently 10% on demand deposits. Thus, even if the earnings credit rate were the same as the organization's short-term investment rate (e.g., assuming that the organization were investing in 90-day t-bills), compensation with balances would be less efficient. For example, an earnings credit rate of 6%, which is approximately .005 on a monthly basis, would only be worth 5.40% (6% times 90%; 100% minus the 10% reserve requirement), or .0045 on a monthly basis.

In the past, some banks have tried to charge a surcharge to companies that choose fee compensation (or a fee-balance combination). This was done to equate the two methods of compensation. However, in recent years, banks, especially the largest ones, are doing this less frequently. They have substituted "tiered" earnings credits to reflect average balances. For instance, a bank may use $250,000 as a cut-off, so any business customer that maintains a balance below this threshold would receive a substantially lower rate than those whose balances were higher.

You may find such charges from banks for parts of your business when banks have different charges based on geographic location. You should try to negotiate standard rates and earnings credit rates with your banks to avoid these charges or lower rates.

Some organizations prefer to compensate with fees because they are explicit and offer tighter cost control. Others prefer balances because they are more flexible. In the past, such balances were sometimes referred to as the treasury manager's shadow budget. This was because many treasury managers were able to purchase services and other bank products without showing them as regular corporate budget items. With fees, of course, this is usually not possible. Some organizations still maintain a portion of their compensation on a balance basis to have this budgetary flexibility.

Fee-balance combination

In reality, most organizations cannot eliminate all their balances and compensate their banks fully on a fee basis. Many banking transactions, especially deposits, generate balances. In addition, corporate disbursements cannot be so finely tuned as to eliminate some balance build-up in the bank. Consequently, organizations seek a compromise with their banks—a fee-balance combination.

Both sides agree that any collected balances generated in the company's bank accounts will first be used to offset bank service charges. The shortfall (assuming that the balances were insufficient) is then made up by paying a fee.

The major drawback to this system is that the balances offset fees at the bank's earnings credit rate (see discussion above), rather than at the customer's short-term investment or borrowing rate. The primary advantage, however, is that the treasury manager does not have to worry about small or accidental balance increases; these are put to use.

It would appear that both sides win with this approach. The organization can titrate its compensation, and, to the extent that it can reduce its balances, it realizes more of the benefits of fee compensation. From the bank's point of view, it receives full compensation regularly, usually monthly. For banks, this may be very attractive as it reduces the need to monitor balance level constantly.

Switch your mind set

Since you will most likely be paying for your service charges by the fee-balance combination discussed above, it is appropriate and advisable for you to focus on fees as much as possible. Of course, you should not ignore balances, but your goal should be to keep them to a minimum. You can do this by dealing with what I call "fee equivalents." By focusing on earnings allowances and fees paid, I think you get a better picture of your compensation. It is not too difficult to do this, but it may mean changing old habits.

Years ago, banks encouraged compensating balances and looked warily at fee payers. This attitude changed as both treasury managers and bankers came to understand the clarity and efficiency of fees. For treasury managers, bank costs are straightforward; for banks, the revenue flow from a customer is easy to measure.

However, if you look at most account analysis statements, you may be surprised to still see a reference to "required" compensating balances. In a section below I will deal with the numbers.

Navigating Your Account Analyses

The document that shows bank balance activity and itemizes monthly bank service charges is the bank account analysis statement. Treasury managers should receive an account analysis (in paper form) from all major corporate banks that shows activity by account on a monthly basis.

Each bank has an individual format for its account analysis, which makes it difficult for treasury managers to compare services and charges among banks. In addition, because many banks have unbundled their service charges to a great degree, their bank account analyses have become lengthy and complex documents.

Despite the existence of many varieties of account analyses, there are several basic items that should appear on all of them, in one form or another. These items are shown in Figure 4-1.

Average balances should tie in to daily averages from the bank's balance reports as long as any adjustments are reflected in the daily reports. Most banks will usually provide a summary of service activity data for all accounts, but this may differ from bank to bank.

Figure 4-1: Basic Features of Account Analyses

Average balances:
These are calculated on an average calendar basis and include ledger, float and collected balances.

Earnings credit:
This is the rate used to value the average collected balance for compensation purposes. It is usually tied to a money market, such as the average 90-day t-bill rate.

Reserve requirement:
This is the rate charged to the bank by the Federal Reserve. It is currently 10%.

Service charges:
These are itemized by account, with a total for each account. These may be shown as charges only, or they may be shown as collected balances required as well.

Settling on fees or balances (or a combination) establishes the framework for bank compensation. On an ongoing basis, you must be able to monitor bank service charges and evaluate them in light of the services received. One of your more productive activities is reviewing the account analyses.

Account analysis reviews

Account analyses, if not already regarded as invoices, are certainly considered as backup support for invoices. This means that verifying the accuracy of the account analyses is not just a mechanical exercise – it is a necessary activity to control banking costs. Errors that are not discovered can create compensation discrepancies. Therefore, a major objective of the review is to verify the accuracy of the statement.

You need to review your account analysis statements as soon as you receive them to identify and correct errors and to challenge "questionable" items appearing on them. Your review should be given a high priority in your work load and should, in any case, be reviewed well before the bank deducts the fee from your bank account. This is what you do with other services; you should do the same for banking services.

Many of the inputs to the account analysis statement are manual reports by bank operating departments. The treasury manager must validate these charges by comparing the volume numbers independently within the organization. This can be done with the person or department responsible for the activity.

Since the account analysis statement is often the basis for a payment, it is important to check the numbers carefully. If it is not feasible to verify the accuracy of each account, comparing charges month to month may be sufficient.

Account analysis statements can also be informative, especially in cases of decentralized systems, because they may report bank activities that the central treasury manager might be unaware of. In this sense, the statements are must readings for the treasury manager.

The analyses may identify inefficient cash management practices (e.g., through the existence of numerous accounts or outdated services being used), duplicate services, and overcompensation or undercompensation. For example, if a service has been changed (e.g., from controlled disbursing to regular disbursing), the account analysis should not continue to show charges associated with the former service (e.g., special account maintenance, clearing notification). Finding several instances like this should be the catalyst for initiating a more formal review. Investigating charges that do not seem to make sense is a good logical approach. In this case it is probably beneficial to question too much, rather than too little.

Errors

The types of error you may encounter are shown in Figure 4-2, along with their causes and typical actions you should take if you encounter them. In most cases, I recommend discussing your findings with your bank right away to make it easier to adjust the fee payment. If you let things drag on, you will have a bigger problem with your bank.

Usually, it is not hard to identify errors like the ones listed. As you spend time reviewing your account analyses, you become more familiar with the typical charges, so the erroneous or suspicious ones will be fairly easy to spot.

If you are not the direct user of the services, you will not be able to judge whether some services you identify as questionable are being used. In such cases, you must rely on local financial managers for review and comment. If this describes your situation, you have even more of a reason to review account analyses as they arrive, distributing them to the appropriate reviewers with your questions and comments. You can then follow up with local managers to determine if any action steps are necessary.

Standardization

For almost two decades, individual companies and the Association of Financial Professionals (AFP) have tried to standardize account analysis statements. The AFP maintains a paper and electronic standard that may help you in reviewing account analysis statements. Most of the large cash management banks have adapted their analyses to agree in some part with the AFP standard, but few banks have totally conformed to the paper standard.

The standard analysis format calls for the analysis document to be divided into sections that cover basic information on the account, such as its number and title, average balances for the

Figure 4-2: Errors on Account Analysis Statements

Error	*Description/Cause*	*Action to Take*
Incorrect volume numbers	Manual posting errors by bank	Instruct bank to revise charges and reflect correction in next account analysis.
Inflated/ deflated volume numbers	Part of last month's volume is included in current analysis, or all of this month's volume is not counted	Monitor months to be sure that volumes overall are being counted accurately.
Incorrect pricing	Unit charges for services are increased without notice	Verify charge increase with bank. If charge violates the service agreement, instruct bank to revise fees charged.
Charges for accounts previously closed	Closed accounts are still shown in analysis package, incurring basic service charges	Instruct bank to eliminate charges and to readjust amount billed.
Charges shown for unknown activity	Charges are shown in error or for services once used but since discontinued	Instruct bank to eliminate charges and to readjust amount billed.
Charges shown in incorrect account	Charge for one account shown in another account's analysis, thereby skewing the charges	If overall charge is still correct, instruct bank as to proper accounts for services; otherwise instruct bank to adjust amount billed.

Figure 4-2: Errors on Account Analysis Statements		
Unknown overdraft charge	Charges shown for ledger and/or collected balance overdrawn when misposting (by bank) created the condition	Instruct bank to eliminate charges and to readjust amount billed.
Incorrect rate charged for overdraft	Rate shown for advanced funds to repay overdraft is higher than the agreed-upon rate	Instruct bank to recompute charges and to readjust amount billed.
Incorrect prices for services	Prices shown are different from those negotiated through RFP or in setting up service	Instruct bank to eliminate charges and to readjust amount billed.

past month and year to date, itemized services charges in summary and by account, details of all adjustments made during the past month, and a management summary of all accounts maintained at the bank. The standard also calls for the detailed services charges to be shown in standard groupings or *families*, such as general services, depository services, information services, etc.

Individual service charges from participating banks are coded numerically to the standard. In this way, corporate treasury managers can compare charges easily. New banks can have their service charge components coded by submitting them to the AFP.

Of course, an account analysis standard may not be necessary for many companies when they roll all their services into one bank. Larger organizations, which are more likely to deal with multiple banks, still face a translation problem in evaluating and comparing bank services. Larger organizations are often more interested in receiving their account analyses electronically to be able to handle them efficiently.

Many treasury work stations offer modules for downloading and reviewing account analyses in electronic format. The standard format has been translated into an electronic data interchange transaction set #822.

If you are interested in a program to help compare and analyze account analyses, there are three products on the market today. They are: SmartAnalysis by Chesapeake Systems Solutions (www.Chessys.com); Bank Fee Analysis by Trintech (www.Trintech.com); and Bank Relationship Manager by the Weiland Financial Group (www.Weiland-wfg.com).

Bank account analyses can be useful in making new service decisions because they contain historical data concerning bank prices. For example, you should use your account analyses to compute average volumes that banks will need when responding to your RFPs. You can also use data derived from your analyses when reviewing bank operating performance.

Baffling Terminology

Do you know what the following terms mean?

> STR Wire - CCM entry, Cashline repetitive, Action rep. outgoing, WDC repetitive wire, Automated FT payment, Wire payment, Wire transfer out - terminal repet., MTS DOM repetitive, WT - repetitive (terminal), FT/PC Fedwire STR thru, DMT - rep/ semi-rep - MACH read-DR.

They all mean *automated repetitive wire transfer*. I think this is a good example of the problems you can face in trying to understand account analyses. In reviewing account analyses, keep a few points in mind:

- *Look for some adherence by the bank to the AFP standard, especially in numeric coding, which may make it possible to translate terms from one bank to another.* Don't expect widespread adherence to the standard yet. The standard does provide standard terms and definitions with cross references among banks to link common terms by standard number. Some banks even show the number on their analyses.

- *Relate all the unbundled charges to the activity with which they are associated.* This may be difficult if you don't understand what the terms mean, so get your banker to define the terms for you. Make notes for future reference, if necessary.
- *Make sure that there are no unexplained charges on the statements.* Flag questionable items for further research and/or discussion with your banker.
- *Spread the wealth.* Involve other treasury staff members in the review. Extra sets of eyes can prove very helpful in detecting errors or in identifying items for further research.

Of course, if you only have one bank, then that's your standard. Then all you have to worry about is understanding the terminology on your analyses. Some banks include a glossary of terms to define their terminology. Next, let's look at how to work with the numbers on the statements.

Working with the Numbers

Try to review your account analyses every month. Use the following points as guidelines for your review:

- **Obtain and review all analyses.**
  If you are not reviewing all analyses at a central level, you're probably overcompensating your banks. Summarize average monthly balances and service charges for the past year. Look for "spikes" in any one month, and be sure to identify what happened and why it happened.
- **Track the total charges monthly.**
  I am continually surprised by how many treasury managers I meet who do not know what they paid for bank services in the past month. You should know this, since it's probably one of the highest expense items for treasury. It is easy to ignore the fee since your bank automatically deducts it from your master account, but this is no excuse for not knowing how much it was.

- **Check the numbers.**
  If the summary sheet for the analyses looks as if it may
  have been or could have been changed, verify that the
  total amount of the service charges equals the amount
  from all the detailed account analyses.
- **Make sure services are actually provided.**
  Hunt for inactive accounts, dormant services,
  unexplained charges, idle balances, and unauthorized
  activities. Confirm all volumes for reasonability and
  accuracy. If you don't know what's reasonable or
  accurate, talk to someone who does.
- **Check analysis statements for unannounced increases
  in service charges.**
  You should refuse to pay for unauthorized or
  unannounced increases.
- **Question any unbundled or line item you don't
  understand.**
- **Review charges and rates for uncollected overdrafts.**
  Make sure that the overdraft was caused by the
  company and not the bank. If the latter, get the charges
  waived.

Using a worksheet

One way to keep track of all this is by using a simple spreadsheet
model, such as the one shown in Figure 4-3. The formulas and
other features of this spreadsheet are straightforward; you do not
need a complex model.

One thing you may wish to do is to put in a conditional test
for the estimated fee payment, so that the answer will be a positive number when a fee is payable and will be zero (or "none")
when no fee is due. This can be done with an "IF" statement in
the Estimated Fee cells that tests to see if the Earnings Allowance
is greater than the Total Service Charges. If it is, then "none" can
be shown as the answer, or if this is not true, then the difference
is shown as a fee payable. Note that "none" is shown for March
on the report.

Figure 4-3 shows three months' actual figures. Note that the
charges jumped in February by almost $500, an increase of 33%

Figure 4-3: Compensation Summary			
	Jan	**Feb**	**Mar**
Main Bank			
Earnings Credit Rate	1.00%	0.90%	1.50%
Reserve Requirement	10.00%	10.00%	10.00%
Average Ledger Balance	$1,250,450	$995,670	$1,275,780
Average Float	$275,000	$289,400	$155,240
Average Collected Balance	$975,450	$706,270	$1,120,540
Earnings Allowance	$744	$453	$1,281
Total Service Charges	$1,456	$1,948	$1,256
Estimated Fee Payment	$712	$1.495	none
Percent Paid in Fees	48.93%	66.37%	0.00%
Note:			
Collected Balances Required for Services	$1,910,022	$2,100,332	$1,098,437
Collected Balance Over/(Under) Required	($934,572)	($1,394,062)	$22,103

over January, and then drop substantially in March. The February jump may be an abnormal increase that could have been caused by an overdraft, an error in volume that included some of March volumes (resulting in a lower charge for March), or a seasonal shift in banking activity.

In any case, the February jump should be investigated further. If it was an *accidental* overdraft that the bank caused by making a misposting in error but forgot to reverse before the analyses were printed, you want to get an adjustment before the fee shown is deducted from your account.

Note that the March figures for balances were more in line with January figures, but the total service charges were down substantially. If the February increase was not explained before the March reports were received, both months could be re-searched at the same time. I would not recommend putting off your investigations that long, since it may be difficult to reconstruct events, volumes, etc. that long after the fact. Investigating while the data are relatively fresh is more effective.

The model shows key figures by month and makes it easy to compare one month's activity with another. Note the following about the report shown in Figure 4-3:

- **The average float figure is deducted from the average ledger balance to yield the average collected balance.** If you incur an overdraft during the month, you may see an adjustment to the average collected balance subtracting "negative collected balances" from the average collected balance total. This is done because your bank has already charged you for the overdraft and to leave the negative number in your average total would be penalizing you twice.

- **The Earnings Allowance value ($744 and $453 for January and February, respectively) is computed by using the following formula, which is an algebraic version of the top portion of an account analysis statement:**

$$EA = (CB) \times [(EC/12) \times (1.00 - RR)].$$

In this formula, EA is earnings allowance, CB is average collected balance, EC is the annual earnings credit rate, and RR is the reserve requirement. Technically, you should use the fraction of the days in the month over the number of days in the year to compute the monthly earnings credit rate, and I used that in this model. However, I have often found it much simpler to divide by 12, as shown in the formula, without changing the final result.

- **The report shows that the percentage paid by fee has changed radically from month to month.**
  This is a result of the large balances maintained and the low earnings credit rate. For example, if the earnings credit rate for January was 2%, the earnings allowance would be $1,487, which would mean that the company would not pay a fee that month.

- **The balances required are shown at the bottom of the report just to keep in mind how much in balances would be tied up to avoid paying by fee.**
  In this way, you do not need to get confused over levels of compensation.

I also suggest that you compute the percentage of total service charges that are paid for by fee, after the offsetting credit for balances maintained. You can see from the figure that this percentage jumped in February due to the increased activity, but tracking this percentage can help keep you motivated to minimize extra balances.

Compensation issues

Even with active balance management, bank compensation may not always be precise, and substantial balances may result. As I said earlier, you may overlook the charges since they are usually deducted directly from your master account and you do not have to approve an invoice to make payment. The "good news" is that charges deducted in this manner seem to be treated differently by corporate budgets; i.e., they do not appear as a line item that is subject to budgetary guidelines or control.

To the extent your balances can reduce or eliminate the monthly fee, they can be put to use. But what if the balances are so high that they more than cover a monthly fee? Depending on the agreement with the bank, most treasury managers would try to negotiate to use these excesses in additional time periods.

Obviously, if this happens infrequently, the negotiation should not be difficult. However, if it happens often, it will be tougher to convince the bank to go along with what appears to be sloppy compensation practices. In such cases, a detailed review of daily cash position and bank target balance management is long overdue.

In cases of undercompensation, you may try to negotiate a longer catch-up period than the current month if the amount is substantially greater than the usual monthly fee. If compensation is by balances or if some or all of the shortfall is to be made up through balances, it is advisable to meet with the bank to mutually agree on a compensation plan that includes amounts, timing and, perhaps, the type of account in which the compensating balance will reside (e.g., in the regular DDA account or in a non-interest-bearing time deposit).

The compensation time frame

Negotiating the compensation horizon, then, is an important part of bank compensation. It is important not only in cases of wide swings in balances but also in the regular monitoring of the company's balances.

The compensation horizon will usually be dictated by the method of compensation. For example, with fee compensation a company will usually agree to a short horizon, often monthly and not longer than quarterly. If a company uses a fee-balance combination, it will also face a similar horizon. These horizons do not seem out of line as they tie payment for service close to the actual delivery of that service.

Companies using balance compensation may find that they can negotiate a longer horizon—from quarterly to annually. This was common in the past, as companies and their banks often monitored compensation on a rolling 12-month basis. The rolling average approach seems to be less common today, and even with compensating balances shorter horizons are becoming more frequent.

Tracking several banks

As bank compensation becomes more complex, it will be useful to monitor the levels of compensation on an ongoing basis. You can use Figure 4-3 if you have only one or two banks. Otherwise, you may want to summarize the information in a simple tracking report. Figure 4-4 shows a report for a company compensating its five banks with a fee-balance combination.

Banks	Ledger ($000)	Collected ($000)	Service Chgs. ($000)	Earnings Allow- ance ($000)	Fees Paid ($000)	Required ($000)
Figure 4-4: Compensation Tracking Report						
Bank A	2,000	1,500	9.9	3.3	6.6	3,000
Bank B	1,400	1,400	11.0	3.1	7.9	3,200
Bank C	1,000	650	13.7	1.2	12.5	3,500
Bank D	500	150	2.0	2.0	0.0	150
Bank E	2,350	1,100	20.2	2.6	17.6	5,100
All Banks	7,250	4,800	56.8	12.2	44.6	14,950

In one case (Bank D), the balances are exactly offsetting the requirements, so no fee has been paid. The collected balance column represents the average collected balance maintained, and this amount is used to calculate the Earnings Allowance (at the bank's earnings credit rate after the 10% reserve requirement has been deducted). These allowances, which represent the "value" of the balances are used as an offset to the charges before the actual fees (shown in the *Fees Paid* column) are remitted.

This type of summary report, which can be set up quickly on a computer spreadsheet, is a helpful management summary. It should be supported by detailed worksheets that use information from each bank's monthly account analyses.

Interest on corporate DDA accounts

Currently, corporations do not earn *explicit* interest on their bank checking accounts. This is prohibited, according to Federal Reserve Regulation Q. There is some debate over whether this ban should be lifted and, if so, what effect the elimination of the ban would have on bank balances and, in turn, bank compensation. Since many companies have reduced the large balances formerly maintained, this is not a big issue for most firms.

Because corporations move funds to concentrate them for investment or other short-term purposes, it is thought that fewer transfers would be required if corporations could earn interest on their checking account balances. This would help in reducing the amount of daylight overdrafts and might simplify many corporate cash management systems. It would also clarify bank compensation, as balances now would earn interest, not earnings credit, although it would probably be possible to select an interest-earning account or a *regular* business account that would not earn interest.

On the other hand, many companies already have approximated this arrangement through the use of bank sweep arrangements. With sweep services, companies have already automaically invested excess balances on a daily basis. Thus, it can be argued that there would be little impact on corporate cash management practices if interest could be earned on corporate accounts.

It should be noted that larger corporations maintaining significant balances that are not currently earning interest are not heavy users of sweep accounts because, it is argued, they are able to obtain better rates on short-term investments than from sweep accounts. However, if they were satisfied with the interest rates offered on regular checking accounts and did not have to pay for funds concentration, they might shift their balances to interest-earning accounts. This shift would have a heavy impact on corporate-bank relations because treasury managers might no longer be concerned about concentrating funds and would redeploy funds from collection points. This could translate into more banking relationships to manage.

Lifting the Unbundling Veil

Many banks have developed intricate and numerous components to describe the charges for cash management services. Often, these seem baffling. How is it possible to understand service charges, let alone compare them?

The best point of understanding is at the time the services are purchased. This is when the seller (i.e., the bank) is or should be willing to "educate" the buyer. Too often, treasury managers do not take advantage of this opportunity.

If you used the RFP process to select a bank to provide your services, you already have had to deal with the different pricing approaches individual banks have adopted. On the other hand, if you got through the RFP process successfully, you learned how to compare charges from one bank to another. To do this you probably had to understand the unbundling to be able to regroup the charges for comparison purposes. I'll call this regrouping "re-bundling."

In Figure 4-5, I show one way to go about comparing costs for the same service between two banks. There can be many components as well as different numbers of them from bank to bank. However, to keep the illustration simple, I have only varied the component costs.

In the figure, the charges for each component are given for the two banks. Note that some are flat fees and others are per item charges. This also complicates comparisons because the final charge may depend on the combination of fixed and variable costs. Since we are applying the same volumes to each, this is not as important a factor as it would be if there were different volumes for each lockbox. In that case, we would need to apply the same volume to each to determine which one offered the better (cheaper) price.

As the figure shows, Bank A shows a lower total charge than Bank X. Had we focused primarily on the per item lockbox processing charge, we might have concluded that Bank X was cheaper. It appears that Bank X's flat charge for the account and its imaging per item charge account for much of the difference in prices. Note that this comparison would get more difficult if additional services were added or if one bank had additional or fewer service charge components.

Figure 4-5: Re-bundling Unbundled Charges					
		Unit Charges		**Service Charges**	
	Vol.	Bank A	Bank X	Bank A	Bank X
Maintenance (flat charge)	1	100.00	125.00	100.00	125.00
Lockbox item processing (per item)	500	0.45	0.42	225.00	210.00
Lockbox photocopy (per item)	500	0.08	0.11	40.00	55.00
Lockbox non-check processing (per item)	50	0.31	0.35	15.50	17.50
Items deposited local Fed (per item)	50	0.11	0.09	5.50	4.50
Items deposited other Fed (per item)	450	0.17	0.15	76.50	67.50
Lockbox imaging (per item, incl. enclosure)	1,000	0.03	0.06	30.00	60.00
Lockbox imaging (flat fee)	1	40.00	35.00	40.00	35.00
ACH debits received (per item)	21	0.10	0.14	2.00	3.00
Data transmission (daily call)	21	0.20	0.25	4.00	5.00
Total charges				**539.00**	**583.00**
Cost per item (total charges ÷ total items)				**1.08**	**1.17**

Overdraft charges are killers!

One of the worst things you can do, in terms of bank service charges, is incur an overdraft. It really does not matter whether you overdraw on a ledger or collected basis (or both). You will pay more for an overdraft than for any other transaction.

Figure 4-6 shows the various rates charged by banks as reported in the 2002-2003 *Phoenix-Hecht Blue Book of Bank Prices*. It shows the median, most frequent, lowest, and highest rates charged for overdrafts. It also shows the prime rate for March for each year. It is interesting to note that the median and highest rates charged were consistently higher than the March prime rate.

Figure 4-6: Rates Charged for Negative Collected Balances (Overdrafts)				
Rates Charged	**1999**	**2000**	**2001**	**2002**
Median	8.75%	11.00%	9.50%	6.75%
Most Frequent	10.75%	12.25%	11.32%	7.75%
Lowest	3.60%	2.75%	4.04%	1.00%
Highest	11.75%	13.00%	12.50%	12.50%
Prime*	7.75%	8.75%	8.50%	4.75%
Prime--Most Frequent	3.00%	3.50%	2.82%	3.00%
*Rate shown is for March of each year				
Source: Phoenix-Hecht Blue Book of Bank Prices, 2002-2003 edition				

Conclusion

Staying on top of your bank costs is one of a treasury manager's most important responsibilities. Yet despite their grumbling about rising costs, you would be surprised at how often in my consulting practice I come across treasury managers who claim to be too busy to check their account analyses. The analyses are piled up, or filed, or in binders, unread for up to a year. Invariably, as I look through them I find all sorts of found money for them. I find straightforward errors in bank charges; bank practices that I wouldn't allow, such as overdraft charges when the combined accounts have high balances; and other symptoms of an inefficient treasury system.

When you have little staff and a lot of responsibilities, it's hard to be punctual about reviewing account analyses and checking your bank compensation. However, I am telling you to revise your priorities. It's worth it.

Chapter 4 ACTION ITEMS

§ Create a spreadsheet model to record monthly service charges and fees paid for each bank. This report should also include the bank's earnings credit rate.

§ Establish a schedule to review monthly bank account analysis statements. Your review should include *all* accounts, services, and banks. Maintain a spreadsheet model to track the following data items:
  • All account analyses received (e.g., show number of accounts) by treasury department
  • Total monthly charges
  • Total charges shown on summary sheet agree with sum of individual account analyses
  • Service charges have not been increased without notification or possibly in violation of a previous service agreement
  • Overdrafts occurred and were handled correctly— amounts, rate charged were correct

Chapter 4 ACTION ITEMS (cont.)

§ Review each bank's account analyses, using Figure 4-2 (descriptions of errors) as a checklist. Resolve any errors within an agreed-upon time period (e.g., 30 days) between your company and the bank. Track errors by bank.

§ Ask each bank for definitions of all terms shown on their account analysis statements. Update this as new terms appear or are added.

§ To avoid costly overdrafts, assure that you have a "cash management" agreement with each bank so that negative balances in one account can be offset by positive balances in another account.

§ Set up and maintain spreadsheet models like those shown in Figures 4-3 and 4-4.

§ For each major activity – e.g., disbursement item, collection/deposited item – compute a rebundled charge, using Figure 4-5 as a guideline. Track these charges over time.

5

Paperwork and Legal Issues

Paperwork is an integral part of any banking relationship. It
starts with the initial arrangements for bank services and continues through individual transactions. In this chapter we discuss
the various forms of documentation and the changing standards
about their use.

Bank/Account Authorization

Treasury managers cannot open bank relationships without
authorization from senior management (the board of directors).
They use one of two approaches to authorize bank relationships.
They either authorize generally—bank by bank—or specifically—
account by account.

The form of the board resolution varies greatly. Most banks
have a standard board resolution form that they will supply.
Many banks insist that their format be the one used. This is especially the case with smaller customers, who often do not have
their own standard forms. However, many organizations do have
their own form and format for board resolutions. In this case, they
supply their documentation to the banks. If the bank's form is
generally the same as the corporation's form, it can be used.

Although the detailed wording may differ slightly from one form to another, the general items do not. They include:

- Name of authorizing person (usually the corporate secretary)
- State of jurisdiction
- Bank name
- Date of resolution
- Titles of authorized signers or persons who can transact the company's business via the bank account
- Official witness and date of signing the resolution.

If the treasury manager is not going to use the bank's format, he or she is usually provided with the board resolution by the corporate secretary. A specific type of resolution would include the type or title of the account to be opened within the quoted resolution.

Because they have to go to their boards to authorize bank or account relationships, treasury managers may sometimes be reluctant to close out all relationships with a bank. By keeping at least one account open, they can resume banking relations without going back to the board for approval.

This means that organizations may hold on to many more bank relations than they actively use. This practice would seem to be risky in that it may appear to violate the spirit of the board authorization. It is something that internal or external auditors might question in their review of treasury operations.

General authorization allows the treasury staff more flexibility and latitude. It also recognizes that the company's board of directors may not be as accessible nor wish to be involved in every bank account decision. Furthermore, in cases where many changes to the banking system are being made or contemplated, individual account authorization can become a bottleneck (e.g., there is a practical limit on how many bank accounts a board can consider at any one time), and the typical monthly cycle for board meetings may create substantial implementation delays (e.g., actions such as ordering checks or notifying customers of a new mailing address may be suspended until the board approves the account). General authorizations are used more often, especially in larger corporations.

Specific account authorization offers the ultimate in control and limits the discretion of the treasury staff in dealing with banks. In situations where changes to bank services are made infrequently, this approach can be practical. Specific authorization is normally used in situations where the board can meet as needed or approve requests by mail or fax. For example, this may apply in the case of a joint venture or wholly owned subsidiary, where it is important that strict control be maintained. Specific authorization is also typical of many smaller companies where senior management functions as the treasury staff and as the board of directors, so the organizations still using this form of authorization may want to convert their resolutions to the general type by changing their by-laws, assuming as they have adequate checks and balances in place.

Operating Procedures

When a corporate treasury manager initially sets up a bank relationship, there are at least three types of standard paperwork involved:

- **Letter of instruction**
  This discusses the purpose of the account and how the bank will handle activity, including such items as normal operating procedures, reporting requirements (e.g., cutoff time for reporting lockbox deposits to the company's concentration bank), special handling or error handling procedures (e.g., what to do with "paid in full" checks received by a lockbox processor or procedures for redepositing returned checks a second time) and the name and title of the primary contact at the company.

- **List of authorized signers**
  This lists the names and titles of all legally authorized signers for the account, usually designating which one(s) will be by facsimile signature (if any) and signed by a senior financial executive, such as the chief financial officer or vice president-treasurer (in

accordance with company by-laws). Depending on the type of account or bank requirement, this list may be accompanied by signature cards containing each authorized signer's signature and specimens of facsimile signatures. Accompanying the list of signatories is usually the company's policy on how many signers are required by type of transaction. For most sizable transactions, two signers are usually required.

- **Board resolution**
  This shows proof of the legal authority for the company to do business with the bank on a form supplied by the bank or the customer and has been completed by the proper corporate officer(s).

Transaction Documentation

In the past, companies confirmed every transaction with their banks. For larger companies with heavy transaction volumes, this meant shipping a mountain of paper daily to their banks. Much of it was to ensure auditability of the systems and reflected the manual nature of many of those systems.

As treasury systems have become more automated and corporate auditors have become more comfortable with bank-corporate information systems (e.g., daily balance reports of detailed debits and credits), many organizations have stopped confirming (in separate written form) transactions between internal company accounts. If you wish to reduce your confirmation activities, you should investigate your organization's current policies regarding confirmations and discuss changes with senior financial management and the company's auditors.

General documentation

There are still activities that should be confirmed by most organizations on a regular basis. These transactions usually involve a third party, such as an investment dealer or foreign exchange trader. In these cases, you use confirmation letters to be sure the transaction details are accurate. For example, reconfirming in writing the interest rate, calculations, and maturity date for a short-term investment offers protection (to both sides) against any surprises at a later date.

For foreign exchange transactions, reconfirming rates and delivery instructions is an important step to assure that the transaction is completed smoothly. Confirmations of such types of transactions are usually customized by each company and include details specific to the transaction.

Other types of banking activities have associated documentation that corporate treasury managers usually handle. These include:

- **Bank loan drawdowns**
  These transactions generally require a note from the company to the bank, signed by authorized signers of the company. It is usually customized by the customer, or a bank-supplied form can be used.

- **Pre-signed notes**
  As an alternative to individual notes, you can sign a note for the full amount of the line. This allows you to draw down on the line as if it were an overdraft facility; i.e., you can draw funds as needed without issuing a new note. In the past, banks offered this capability by using grid notes. These were used when heavy borrowing, usually on a daily basis, was anticipated. There is a master grid note, on which the bank records daily loan transactions. This is renewed periodically.

- **Commercial paper notes**
  Banks serve as issuing agents for corporate commercial paper, which used to require the borrowing firm to provide the issuing bank with a supply of pre-signed notes by the corporation's authorized signer(s). This arrangement has largely disappeared due to the shift to paperless commercial paper.

- **Other technical forms**
  These include specialized forms for specific types of transactions. An example is a MICR (magnetic ink character recognition) specification sheet that many banks supply for ordering check stock.

Special requests

Treasury managers handle other forms of documentation less frequently than the types discussed above. One of these is the annual confirmation of bank services for audit purposes. This is usually undertaken as part of the annual financial audit by the company's public accounting firm. There are generally two items that the company's auditors want to confirm for each bank. The first is any credit facility provided by the bank. You send out forms supplied by your auditor to each bank that provides a line of credit or other credit facility (e.g., a revolving credit facility). Responses are sent directly to the auditors. This information, in summary form, usually appears as a footnote to the company's financial statements.

The other item to be confirmed is an account and loan balance. Forms are typically provided by your outside auditors. Just as with the credit confirmation, you send the forms to your bank with instructions to return the completed confirmation directly to the auditor.

Finally, some documentation may be required from the bank on an ad hoc basis. Usually, these are check copies in cases of legal or payment disputes. Also, companies undertaking collection or disbursement studies may ask their banks for extra copies or additional details during a study period.

Service Agreements

Companies and banks may also sign bank service agreements. There are different levels of service agreements, starting with standard legal agreement that banks require their corporations to sign so that both sides are protected from unlawful movements of funds from the company's account.

Companies may expand the concept of a service agreement beyond what they receive from the bank to create a binding document between the company and the bank. Figure 5-1 lists key items to consider in an expanded service agreement.

You can use a service agreement to document your compensation, performance measurement, and pricing negotiations with the bank. For example, you could ask your banks to agree to a fixed price for a service, a fixed level of price increases over a de-

Figure 5-1: Checklist of Key Items for Bank Service Agreements

Operating procedures
- Are all procedures understood (by the bank) and documented?
- Are exception situations identified?
- Are company contacts for these situations provided?
- Are regular contacts provided?

Reporting requirements
- Are proper addresses provided?
- Are reporting cutoffs clearly stated?
- What if there is no activity on a day?
- What about company holidays? Bank holidays?

Performance measurement standards
- Have service quality standards been agreed to by the bank?
- Can they be regularly collected and reported?
- Who will be in charge of this?
- Have any new standards been used, or will they be available in the near future?

Liabilities and indemnification
- Do any service agreements conform to the UCC?
- If not, has corporate counsel signed waivers?
- How will damages be identified and handled?
- At what rate will lost funds be reimbursed?

Compensation
- How will the bank be compensated for this account— balances, fees, or combination?
- How long is the compensation period? Monthly? Quarterly? Longer?
- Is this account tied into an overall corporate summary?

(continued)

Figure 5-1: Checklist of Key Items for Bank Service Agreements (cont.)

Ability to audit
- Does the company have explicit authority to visit the bank?
- Do its auditors?
- Does it have any restrictions on access to corporate data or other materials?

Notifications
- How much lead time must there be for notifications of change or termination?
- Are all changes in procedure and in the service required to be in writing?

Authorized activities
- Are all activities (i.e., transactions into and out of the account) defined?
- Does this include and/or preclude preauthorized transactions, such as ACH debits?

Authorized persons
- Are all authorized signers current?
- Are any signers to be restricted in any way, or can any signer initiate or confirm any type of authorized transaction?

Document flow
- Is the expected flow of documents (both ways) defined?
- Is each document identified sufficiently such that either side can understand its source and disposition?

fined period of time, or a flexible price depending on how well the bank provided service (a standard work order).

Many banks have resisted agreeing to a standard work order, but pressure from customers may change this. These documents tend to be customized by the situation and relationship between customer and bank, and, unlike the standard service agreement mentioned above, this agreement is usually drawn up by the customer for the bank to sign.

This event should not be a surprise for the bank; the bank and the customer should have agreed beforehand that a service agreement of this sort was part of establishing the service. Arrangements like this are common in situations where formal requests for proposal have been used.

Documentation

Another key piece is bank documentation. This includes an up-to-date listing of contacts. You may want to ask your banker to give you an organization chart or e-mail list so you can contact key people directly. You'll want to keep an electronic card file and copies of board resolutions and bank operating agreements.

Figure 5-2 shows a standardized form, which I call the Bank Book. It can be used as a template for standardized documentation. You can use the Bank Book to document existing relationships when you deal with multiple banks. It can also be used to document overseas banking services with some slight modifications (in terminology). Your main bank or an outside consultant can help you with some of the terms, if you need assistance.

When companies add to or otherwise modify service arrangements, the treasury manager usually handles the paperwork. This adds another responsibility for the treasury manager—monitoring and maintaining the list of authorized signers and related items, such as facsimile signature plates, which may be used by every operating location that issues pay checks or prints disbursement checks locally.

In a large corporation with many local operations, this can be a time-consuming task, especially if there is much turnover in authorized signers. It also becomes a concern when mergers or sales of operations are involved. The inventory of signature plates and authorized signing authority are items that are usually reviewed annually by the company's internal and external auditors.

Figure 5-2: The Bank Book

Bank Name:	Corp. Master Acct. #
Location:	

Credit Services ($Millions)

	HQ	Div A	Div B	Sub A	Sub B	For Sub X	For Sub Y
Regular (committed) line							
Revolving credit agreement							
Term loan							
Letter of credit							
Foreign loan facility							
TOTAL							

Non-Credit Services

Lockbox							
OTC deposits							
ACH concentration							
Controlled disbursement							
Regular disbursement							
Payroll							
Information reporting							
Wires							
Foreign exchange							
Custody							

Bank Compensation

	Services			
	Credit		Non-Credit	
Time Period (Qtr. or Month)	Fees	Avg. Coll. Bal.	Fees	Avg. Coll. Bal.
Current qtr/month				
Previous qtr/month				
Two qtrs/mos ago				
Three qtrs/mos ago				
This qtr/mo. one year ago				

Figure 5-2: The Bank Book (cont.)			
Contacts			
Role	*Name*	*Title*	*Tel. No.*
Senior			
Contact			
International			
Other Information:			
Sub A President on Board			

UCC 3, 4 and 4A Considerations

One other cross-check in establishing bank accounts is to review bank agreements for conformity with Uniform Commercial Code (UCC) Articles 3, 4, and 4A. With new changes to these articles pending or already implemented in many states, you should have your legal counsel review all legal documentation with your main bank(s) before any documents are accepted.

The UCC articles cited above govern the basic law behind paper-based and electronic payments. Electronic funds transfer (Article 4A) sets forth the legal liabilities and responsibilities of banks and their customers. Banks and their customers can agree to a contract (e.g., in the form of a service agreement) that over-rides basic UCC coverage. Organizations therefore should review what the UCC protections are (by checking with their legal counsel) before completing negotiations for new bank services.

A specific UCC-related issue is when a check has two different amounts on it, one in numbers and one written out. This is what UCC Article 3 refers to as "Contradictory Terms." The actual language is shown in the following excerpt (taken from the Web site that contains all articles of the UCC – law.cornell.edu):

> "§ 3-114. CONTRADICTORY TERMS OF INSTRUMENT
>
> If an instrument contains contradictory terms, typewritten terms prevail over printed terms, handwritten terms prevail over both, and words prevail over numbers."

Note the last phrase – "words prevail over numbers." This means that the written terms – i.e., the written-out dollar amount – are the legal amounts. There have been discussions to change this, but (as of 2004) this has not yet happened.

Conclusion

Paperwork is an inevitable component of managing banking relationships. Authorizations, operating procedures, transaction documentation, and service agreements must all be documented and kept current. The legal ramifications are obvious. A final note of caution: Don't forget that no matter what you think you and your bank have agreed to in terms of service or compensation, you have no grounds for complaint if you have no documentation to back you up.

Chapter 5 ACTION ITEMS

§ Maintain a "current" listing of authorized signers, signature cards, and board resolutions (if specific to account) for all company bank accounts. This should be kept in one central place and can be kept as electronic images, if desired.

§ Design a general bank board resolution, getting legal clearance from company legal staff and/or outside counsel. Use this as a template for new banking arrangements that do not require a specific account resolution.

§ Design a specific bank board resolution (e.g., for a lockbox account), getting legal clearance from company legal staff and/or outside counsel. Use this as a template for new banking arrangements that call for specific account resolutions.

§ Develop a standard instruction letter (use as boiler plate for new services).

§ Develop a list of transactions that must be documented, using the list below as a guide. Show how documentation is to be handled.
  • Funds transfers (wires, ACH)
  • Loan drawdowns and repayments
  • Transaction notes for loans, commercial paper, etc.
  • Other (specify)

Chapter 5 ACTION ITEMS (cont.)

§ Using Figure 5-1 as a checklist, document the items shown for each major bank service, such as controlled disbursements, lockbox, etc. Maintain records on a spreadsheet model.

§ Create your bank book, along the lines of Figure 5-2. This will require research and regular updating.

§ Conduct an annual UCC review, focusing on Articles 3 and 4 to determine if any changes have been made.

6

Measuring Performance

In any working relationship, it is appropriate to agree on some level of performance measurement. This is especially true in corporate-bank relationships because the relationship is founded on service. Measuring the quality of bank services can be too subjective if the proper framework for performance is not established. Furthermore, evaluating the bank's financial stability is another part of a treasury manager's responsibilities. In this chapter, I discuss approaches to performance measurement and present some alternatives.

Operating performance

In a very basic sense, you could use the satisfaction levels of company personnel who deal with the bank to measure the quality of the bank's performance. This does not help you, however, in managing bank relations because it is not sufficiently objective or quantitative.

Using bank measures

One way to establish appropriate benchmarks is to use what the service providers—the banks—use internally. With some adaptations, bank measures may be a tool you can use. However, this may not work effectively because the bank's standards are not customer-oriented; they are oriented toward measuring bank employee performance.

In the past, many banks held customer "round tables" to review how well the bank was performing and to inform the bank's customers on bank quality improvements. Many of these programs seem to have been put on the shelf, so obtaining service quality information may be difficult.

Developing measures

Performance measurement is becoming more commonplace in treasury. Measures can be quantitative and/or qualitative, and the data to develop the measure have to be readily available. Also, the frequency of measurement—ongoing vs. one-time—must be agreed upon.

To establish a proper framework, you, your staff, and your bankers should work out appropriate performance measures and how they will be applied. This usually entails developing operating benchmarks derived from some unit of activity, such as an item (check, wire transfer) processed or deposited, or an action, such as notification of controlled disbursement clearings, lockbox concentration call, or a bank information report.

Figure 6-1 shows some typical performance measures for treasury management activities. These are examples of standards that can be used internally or externally (i.e., with your banks) as benchmarks for measuring each of the activities shown. Of course, you should use this as a starting point and customize the standards to your need.

In applying standards to measure performance, you should be sure to maintain an objective perspective and to measure activities in the long term, not in the short term. Also, it may not be realistic to beat the benchmark; maintaining performance within tolerances, such as ±5% may be perfectly acceptable. The keys to making an operating performance measurement system work are the acceptance of the benchmarks by both sides, objective collection of the data and periodic review of the performance results.

Figure 6-1: Performance measurement standards

Activity	*Standard*
Short-term investing	Short-term money market rate, such as 90-day US Treasury bill or comparable instrument for each overseas market, obtained from standard source routinely
Short-term borrowing	Short-term bank rate (matched by maturity), Federal Reserve composite rate available from NY Fed, or standard rates (from banks) for overseas locations
FX trades	Use standard daily rates from independent source, such as Reuters, major trading bank, interbank rate, Wall Street Journal, et al.
FX exposure management	Gain or loss vs. plan, or create hypothetical result from 100% unhedged position
Cash management studies	Improvement in bank balances freed up, valued at company's cost of capital on annual basis, fees reduced by implementing study, overseas: reduced bank credit line usage, etc. (Might depend on consultant's estimate)
Bank compensation	Excess balances not utilized, or average fees vs. plan or vs. historical average
Risk management	Gain or loss vs. plan, or create hypothetical result from 100% unhedged position

The report card concept

In the past, when many organizations used multiple banks for cash management and other services, they adopted a measurement system for bank performance that included issuing quarterly *report cards* to their banks. These report cards came in many varieties, but they generally were set up to measure and compare similar services provided by multiple banks. With the continued reduction in the number of banks organization use, the comparative nature of report cards became irrelevant because many organization only used one bank for most services.

However, the *concept* of a report card is not irrelevant. Using an approach similar to Figure 6-2 can help establish an objective appraisal of a bank's performance. The card shown uses the standard technique of grading on a scale of 1 to 5, with 5 being the highest score. Each service is scored, using the rating system that assigns scores based on problems experienced during the past period. In addition, if the bank has provided service above average or less than average—but without problems, its rating can be upgraded or downgraded accordingly. This leaves a little room for general good or bad impressions.

The report card in Figure 6-2 shows the bank's scores for the current period, last period, and a rolling five-period average. This is done to allow easy comparisons from period to period and to a longer range. For instance, the wholesale lockbox service seems to be improving since its current ranking was 4, which is higher than last period (3) and the rolling average (3.5). Note that the rolling average can be set for any number of periods.

When to use report cards

Report cards should be used constructively to resolve problem areas and improve service quality and delivery. Since they take some time to prepare, they do not have to be completed frequently. A semiannual or quarterly cycle is probably sufficient.

The report card can also be used to suggest topics for discussion with your bank at regularly scheduled bank meetings. For instance, you could send the report card to the bank prior to the meeting, noting that any services receiving a score of 3 or lower would be scheduled for discussion. Obviously, you will need to be able to back up the score with details.

Figure 6-2: Bank Report Card

Services	Current period	Last period	Rolling Avg.*
Bank: Bank X			
Controlled Disbursements	5	5	5.0
Wholesale Lockbox	4	3	3.5
Retail Lockbox	5	4	4.0
Wire Transfer	3	4	3.3
ACH Concentration	4	5	4.2
Balance Reporting	4	4	4.0
ST Investments	4	2	3.5
Credit Line	5	3	4.0
Account Analysis	3	4	3.3
Positive Pay	4	4	4.0
Direct Deposit of Payroll	5	4	4.2
ACH Services	3	3	3.0
Bank Average	4.1	3.8	3.8

*Average for last five periods

Bank(s) rated on the following scale:

5: No problems during the time period

4: One major problem and/or up to three minor problems

3: Up to five problems, with no more than two major ones

2: Five to ten problems, with no more than two major ones

1: More than two major problems

(NA – service not provided)

Note: General service performance may add or subtract from bank's rating.

Major problems are those that take more than one day to resolve and require interaction by a higher level manager.

If you use more than one bank for cash management services, you can issue separate or combined report cards. A separate one might be a better idea, unless the banks are providing equivalent services. Otherwise, the bank scores would not really be comparable.

You could use the report cards on an internal basis only as a means of monitoring bank performance, but I think that would be an inefficient use of the concept. It makes sense to share your findings and impressions with your service providers.

Previous report cards can be used to determine whether to initiate the process for competitive bidding for the company's services. A general level of dissatisfaction, as evidenced by lower score on the report cards, may help you identify the services that need improvement. Remember, however, that you are grading the bank or banks primarily on problems, and you should be sure not to penalize any bank if the problem was created by the company, not the bank.

Rating banks

Another report card technique that can be used when considering the banks to include in a bank selection project (using RFPs or not) is to ask a group of company managers to rank potential banks on several attributes. An illustration of this concept is shown in Figure 6-3.

In this approach, you rank current or potential banks according to several attributes, each of which is given a subjective weight. Each bank's rank is then multiplied by the attribute's weight, and these products are added up. The banks with the highest totals or with totals equal to a threshold score (e.g., 70 points) would be considered for inclusion in an RFP project.

The simplified model shown in the figure rates the banks on ten attributes. Each attribute is given a weight (on a one-to-three scale) by consensus among appropriate corporate personnel. Each bank is then rated (on a one-to-five scale) on each attribute by the group that assigned the weights. The final scores are shown on the report.

The final rating for each bank on each attribute could be the average of all the raters. If many banks are being rated this way,

Figure 6-3: Rating Banks						
Attributes	**Weight**	**Bank A**	**Bank B**	**Bank C**	**Bank D**	**Bank E**
Operating performance	3	15	12	9	15	12
Problem-solving	2	8	8	8	10	6
Innovativeness	3	12	9	9	15	12
Willingness to customize	2	6	10	8	6	4
Accuracy	2	10	8	10	10	10
Service costs/prices	3	9	9	15	12	6
Technical capabilities	3	15	12	12	15	9
Market position	1	5	4	4	5	2
Responsiveness	2	6	6	8	8	4
Flexibility	1	3	5	3	3	4
Total Score		**89**	**83**	**86**	**99**	**69**

Note: Banks are rated 1-5 (5 is highest; weights are assigned 1, 2, or 3 (3 is highest)

Scores shown are the products of a bank's rating and weight of attribute.

the computations can be done easily on a computer spreadsheet. In this example, Bank D earned the highest score, based on its high ratings for operating performance, innovativeness, and technical capabilities. If these banks were being considered for an RFP project and the "cutoff" score was 70, then the first four banks would qualify, while the fifth, Bank E, would be eliminated.

Note that with this approach you do not have to base your ratings on actual experience. You could award scores based on research with other firms or outside experts (e.g., consultants). Whatever method is used, you and other raters must try keep an objective, consistent approach. Applying a quantitative measure to what is usually a qualitative area can help you make better decisions.

Periodic bank reviews

As I mentioned earlier, I believe one of the key activities in successful corporate bank relations is effective communications between the organization and the bank. Whether the treasury manager prepares a report card or not, the benefit of regular feedback between service provider and service user is invaluable. This is usually accomplished during a regular call on the treasury manager by the banker. If more important issues or substantial problems are to be discussed, a special meeting should be scheduled.

In the past, regular meetings have focused on more than just operating problems. Discussion topics included items such as possible short-term financial needs and the customer's financial performance (recent or anticipated). Today's meetings are likely to add the bank's financial performance. The outcome of these meetings is a better understanding of the needs of both sides and some assistance in planning for future activities. The bank should be able to determine how it's doing and what new resources it will have to bring to the company to meet the new needs the company has discussed.

It is possible, of course, that there will be no new business in the immediate future; this will be evident from the results of the meeting. The company comes away from the meeting with a better understanding of the bank's commitment and a better sense of what capabilities the bank has.

Meeting with several banks

Sometimes, a corporation may need to meet with more than one banker at a time. On these "show and tell" occasions, a formal meeting is planned with a prearranged agenda. Even if you are meeting with one or just a few banks, it helps to have an agenda. A sample agenda might contain the following general discussion items:

- Company financial results — latest quarter
- Company financial results — projected
- Industry outlook — company's main business lines
- Company future business plans, product introductions
- Specific financial plans — role of the company's banks
- Specific non-credit service needs, changes.

Holding a meeting of this sort takes a great deal of time and effort. It is typically held near the corporate headquarters or at a major operating facility. If at the latter, a plant tour and a product demonstration are often included in the program.

You should consider your banks to be an interested audience. Typically, senior members of the bank - those with the highest level of customer responsibility - are invited to attend the meeting. Senior financial and executive managers of the company are also expected to participate. The purpose of the meeting, which all senior managers of the corporation should understand, is to deliver a strong message to the company's banks. This message is usually that the company has turned around a bad situation or is faced with a particularly bad situation and needs help. Rarely is a meeting held just to say that things are all right and are going to continue that way.

Bankers will want to know how the company is doing financially and what to expect over the near term. After reviewing the company's performance, most companies offer a picture of their major business lines as well. This establishes the company's role in its industries and, in cases of industry-wide malaise, helps explain the company's financial performance. Next, the company reports on new developments - mergers, new product lines, planned investments. This lays the groundwork for discussing financial and non-credit service needs - where the banks can help.

Treasury Reviews

When you are faced with restructuring banking services, you may often need to conduct a comprehensive review of treasury operations to identify and understand problems and service needs more fully. Figure 6-4 offers a checklist of items to be considered in a typical review. During the review process, you will probably

Figure 6-4: Treasury Review Checklist

Part 1: Treasury Organization Review

How static or dynamic has the treasury function been (e.g., have there been any mergers recently)?

What are the specific functional areas within the treasury function? How long has treasury handled them? Have there been any changes recently?

How long has the treasury function been (de)centralized? How does this affect other financial areas? Any problems?

Where is the treasury function located (i.e., where does it report)? How does treasury influence company actions?

How important is the treasury function to the overall company? Is it considered a valuable member of the financial team? Does it play a leading role in financing, or does it trail events?

How does the treasury function relate to other financial units? How does it interact with budgeting and planning, general accounting, accounts receivable, accounts payable and inventory management?

How important is technology to treasury? How automated are treasury systems and support functions?

Who handles changes or upgrades to treasury systems? How involved is treasury with EDI and financial EDI?

How global is treasury? Will this change in the future? What effect(s) will global developments have on treasury?

(continued)

Figure 6-4: Treasury Review Checklist (cont.)

Part 2: Cash Management Practices

When was the last time you reviewed your cash management system in detail, challenging all banking services and relationships?

When was the last time you did a collection study? What is the length of your collection float?

When was the last time you did a disbursement study? What is the length of your disbursement float?

How dependent are you on paper-based processing vs. electronic? Are there areas that could be converted?

Do you use wire transfers to concentrate funds? If so, why and how often? Could they be converted to ACH?

How accurate and/or reliable is your short term forecasting? Medium- to long-term forecasting? What steps could you take to improve any or all of these forecasts?

How automated is your cash management/treasury system? Do you use off-the-shelf software? How old is the system? Has it been reviewed for technical currency recently?

Do you receive account analyses regularly from all major banks? Are they reviewed as soon as they are received? How well have you managed your bank compensation?

Could you use bank report cards or some form of objective appraisal of bank operating performance in your regular operating procedures?

Are you involved in international operations? Should you consider country reviews or other international studies?

make a number of decisions that affect your banking services. The net result should be a simplification of the company's banking network and greater operating efficiencies.

One of the results of a major treasury management review is a detailed description of the bank services used by the company. Whether this is the final system or a new one is subsequently established, there is substantial value in developing and maintaining a master bank book.

Figure 5-2 in the previous chapter gives an example that can be used as a master template. This takes some effort to complete initially, but, thereafter, it can be a valuable resource. Here, in one place is the full spectrum of activity with each bank. Anyone involved with bank relations, from the most senior executive to the smallest staff person, can readily see how important any bank is to the company. Senior executives can prepare quickly for a meeting with their counterparts from the bank. Treasury managers at a subsidiary can see the other services the bank is providing to the company and, perhaps, consider contacting the bank to do the same for their operation. The central corporate treasury manager can review the full scope of activities with each bank and evaluate the contribution of each of the company's major banks.

Bank Financial Ratings

In the past, companies took bank stability for granted. After a number of major banking problems, however, companies grew more concerned about the ability of their banks to be reliable resources. From an analytical perspective, there are several factors that determine how solid a bank is financially and how successful it might be in the future. Financial analysts evaluate a bank's profitability and loan-loss exposure from current and potential high-risk sources (e.g., developing countries, real estate) and look for strengths, such as diversification—by industry or by geography —as important criteria in evaluating a bank.

Treasury managers should monitor changes in the long-term and short-term ratings of their banks from a major credit rating firm (e.g., Moody's, Standard & Poor's, etc.) or from an investment bank that follows the industry. Many of these services are available free or for a small subscription charge. If more detail is necessary, all the major rating agencies and several specialized firms offer additional services for a fee.

Dealing with banks in trouble

In recent years, corporations have been looking just as hard at the financial performances of their banks as the banks have been looking at theirs. Shifting gears from an operational mind set is difficult, but corporate treasury managers have been and will most likely be continued to be called upon to justify their choice of banks. With the current concern for safety, corporate treasury managers may decide that some banks are "safe," while others offer too big a risk.

If a bank has financial difficulties, it is possible that it may also have difficulties in delivering consistent, cost-effective products on an ongoing basis. In addition, the financial commitment (and, in turn, the operational commitment) of the bank to any single service or group of services may be diminished by the need to support other services.

Banks seldom get into financial or operational trouble overnight. Ratings downgrades, profitability decline, and service fall-off are telltale signs. What should a company do? As part of your monitoring activities, you should raise the issue with senior treasury and (possibly) financial management to decide whether the company should continue to do business with the bank.

You should consider the bank's financial situation and expected developments. Also, you have to consider the length and strength of the company's past relationship with the bank. If the decision is made to discontinue business with the bank, you probably should act quickly.

FDIC coverage

One of the more complex issues is FDIC coverage. The current insurance limit is $100,000 per account. However, corporations may discover that this does not apply to each of their accounts individually; it may apply to an aggregation of some or even all of their accounts.

The FDIC recognizes a separate bank depositor as an entity that is engaged in an *independent* activity. This is to prevent a company from spreading out its deposits in many accounts to avoid exceeding the insurance limit. The account holder has to be a separate legal entity, which most wholly owned subsidiaries are but operating divisions are not. The FDIC assesses the purpose of the account and whether any fiduciary relationship exists between the company and the beneficiary of the funds. If it finds an arm's length relationship, those funds will probably be considered as a *separate right and capacity* from other company operating accounts (e.g., regular checking account, lockbox depository account or company benefit plan). It also helps to define the fiduciary relationship explicitly in the name of the account.

If the decision is made to continue with the bank, you will have to continually monitor and report on the bank until the situation improves. You should develop contingency plans in case further deterioration occurs to be able to act quickly to protect the organization's assets.

Chapter 6 ACTION ITEMS

§ Using Figure 6-1 as a checklist, create a spreadsheet model to compute and monitor monthly or quarterly performance "metrics" for each major activity (mark any activities that do not apply as "N/A"):
   • Short-term investing
   • Short-term borrowing
   • FX trades
   • FX exposure management
   • Cash management studies
   • Bank compensation
   • Risk management.

Chapter 6 ACTION ITEMS (cont.)

§ Investigate any metric (as described in the preceding item) that changes by more than a specified percentage (e.g., +/- 10%). Modify metric as necessary.

§ Establish a regular (quarterly) bank performance report, using Figure 6-2 as a guide. This can be done using a spreadsheet model.

§ For prospective banks, use the approach shown in Figure 6-3 to gauge existing attitudes toward the bank.

§ Conduct a treasury (and banking) review at least every 3-5 years or whenever there has been a major change in organization (e.g., acquisition, spin-off, bank consolidation).
  • Use the treasury checklist shown in Figure 6-4 to create your own, more customized review
  • Do this type of review before initiating any service selection project.

7

Strategies and Policies

It is difficult to function effectively without some idea of what your goals are. To establish achievable goals, you need an effective bank strategy and policies to support the strategy. Your strategy can encompass day-to-day activities as well as long-term objectives.

Establishing a Bank Strategy

Why do you need strategies and policies? A primary reason is to provide an overall framework for your bank relationships. In addition, when you select banking services, you are functioning as a purchasing (or supply chain) manager. Therefore, you need to be sure you approach banking services as a supply chain (i.e., a financial supply chain). This forces you to function within limits and to work with guidelines and policies to help in making service decisions.

If an organization has a strategy for investing or borrowing, shouldn't it also have one for bank non-credit services? If one already exists for banks in general, shouldn't it be expanded to include all bank services?

For instance, some organizations have formal, inclusive policies regarding their cash management or treasury activities. I think bank relationship management should be a part of this overall policy.

Developing a Comprehensive Bank Policy

Before developing a detailed bank policy, the designers of the policy should agree on a statement of the corporation's objectives or philosophy with regard to bank relations. This statement could include how the banks fit into the company's short-term and long-term financial plans and strategies—for example, the company may be a net borrower and must depend on its banks for continual short-term loans or backup for the company's commercial paper program. It could also include how bank services are to be obtained—for example, the company may intend to obtain cash management services that are reasonably priced. All aspects of the bank policy should be written, and, when finished, the policy should be formally approved by senior management.

Grouping banks

If an organization has numerous bank relationships, it is often effective to group the banks together in tiers or service levels. The policy should also formally define the requirements for inclusion in each group. The top group could include major banks, such as a main credit and operating banks, as well as other banks that provide a defined level or number of non-credit services or a minimum level of credit. A second-tier group could include banks providing single services, ranging from credit to payrolls or local plant disbursements, or banks that are part of a company network, such as those banks only providing a lockbox service or that only receive field location deposits.

Figure 7-1 is a checklist of items to consider in formulating a bank policy. It is useful to categorize issues into three major categories. The categories and related major issues are shown in the figure.

Figure 7-1: Cash Management Policy Issues

Bank Relations
  Bank level of importance
  Identification of bank "stability" parameters
  Bank operating performance measurement
  Measurement parameters
  Bank compensation
  Method
  Time horizon
  Procedures for daily bank balance and cash
    position management
  Internal (company) responsibilities for bank
    communications
  Internal responsibilities for bank relationship
    management
  Time periods for regular bank review

Short-term Liquidity Management
  Investment policy guidelines
  Investment custody and safekeeping guidelines
  Borrowing policies & documentation
    standards
  Foreign exchange trading and timing guidelines
  Foreign exchange exposure & hedging guidelines
  Derivatives and other risk management guidelines

Treasury Organizational Items
  Use of consultants
  Use of outside managers (e.g., money managers,
    pension managers)
  Use of requests for proposals
  Responsibilities for bank relationship management
  Responsibilities for bank communications
  Bank documentation standards
  Personal banking guidelines

Compensation policy items

The bank policy should cover several compensation items. This might include the method of compensation to be used for various types of services or general guidelines in selecting the compensation method. For instance, you may want to have a policy of paying fees for cash management services unless there are "residual" collected balances that cannot be eliminated in the company's bank account. This type of statement can provide guidance to the treasury manager when he or she is considering changing compensation.

The policy can also formally incorporate bank service charges (fees or fee equivalents if balances are used) into the organization's budgeting process. In some cases, bank charges may fall outside the budget process because they were not considered as managed cost items. Even if this is the situation at your organization, you should describe the budgetary impact of bank charges in the bank policy.

Another compensation item to be addressed is the desired horizon for bank compensation or guidelines for negotiating the proper horizon. In the past, banks and their customers often agreed to a *rolling* yearly average (i.e., a continual yearly average), at least for most cash management services. This has changed in recent years as more organizations have shifted away from total compensation by balances. As a result, the compensation horizon has required redefinition and, usually, has been narrowed.

Today, the common horizons for compensation for cash management services are monthly or quarterly. Credit services that require ongoing compensation, such as lines of credit or revolvers, may be included in the same compensation horizon as cash management services, especially if excess operating balances are going to be used for credit compensation.

Target balance policy items

Even when compensation is primarily in the form of fees, you will probably discover that you must maintain some level of balances at your major operating bank to avoid costly overdrafts and to accommodate last-minute cash needs. In other words, some balances will always remain at these banks. An average level of these

118

residual balances should be your target—i.e., the average balance you try to maintain.

Procedures for maintaining daily bank target balance levels should also be part of the bank policy, even if the target is zero. Assuming that you will have residual balances, you should assure that they are included in an overnight sweep arrangement to earn interest on these dormant balances.

The policy may also specify how often targets should be reviewed and/or updated, as well as how much below or above a target you can be without exceeding a performance measurement benchmark. This latter limit is intended to prevent wide swings in balances, which occur when you try to bring average balances maintained in line with your target quickly (e.g., in a few days).

Other policy items

The policy can identify who is responsible for major activities. For example, it can show the title of the person or the department responsible for primary bank communications. This helps others in the company know who is in contact (or who is supposed to be in contact) with the company's banks.

The list of responsibilities can also include other aspects of the company's bank relationship management, such as the persons or departments responsible for negotiating credit services, maintaining bank account documentation, and monitoring bank operating and financial performance.

Finally, the policy should specify the time period for regular bank review. Meeting regularly with major banks is an effective technique to assure regular interaction. This may take the form of an annual bankers' meeting, often at a major operating location. Dealing with this specifically in the bank policy assures that the meetings will receive the appropriate attention from all those involved with managing bank relations.

Review of bank policy

Like any other policy, the bank policy will benefit from the feedback of everyone involved in bank relations. Therefore, it is advisable to circulate a draft of the policy as it nears completion.

The circulation list will vary from company to company, but it should encompass all those who deal with the company's banks, not just treasury personnel. This list should include senior financial management, the accounting department, internal audit (possibly) and local financial managers, if the company has a decentralized cash management system. Final approvals should come from the treasurer and the chief financial officer.

The policy may also specify how often it is to be reviewed for possible update. Typically, this should occur annually, but there may be occasions when this timetable is too long (e.g., in the case of a major acquisition or sale of an operating unit).

The bank policy should be an active, usable document. It should be one of the fundamental training tools for newly hired or recently promoted treasury managers. In other words, it ought to be "must" reading for anyone new to corporate treasury. If it is sufficiently comprehensive, it is a perfect starting point for internal or external auditors who wish to understand and review the company's banking system. It can also serve as the proper reference to resolve disputes over any aspect of bank relationship management.

The Daily Routine: Managing the Cash Position

One of your daily tasks as a treasury manager is managing the balances in your main bank accounts, which may be with one or more major banks. As described in your bank policy, you should use history to establish a realistic target balance level for each bank.

Monthly bank account analysis statements and average daily balance levels over an adequate period of time are what you use to set your target balance levels. However, don't set them and forget them. Targets should be reviewed regularly to make sure they are still reasonable.

On a daily basis, you monitor the balances in the bank and adjust them upward or downward as necessary. The adjustment is usually made through a transfer into or out of a control account, which is usually your general or concentration account with the bank.

If targets are not monitored daily, large deficits or excesses may result. In such cases, substantial funds transfers may be necessary to get back to the average target, and you may incur costly overdrafts as well.

An example

Figure 7-2 shows the type of data received daily by the treasury manager, typically through the bank information reporting system. In this case, balances from the company's main bank are all that is necessary.

We can assume that the starting balance is shown as the first thing on Monday's column – $50,000. However, on Tuesday, the balance has increased to $70,158, and the report shows the same balance for Tuesday through Friday. The balance will change as each prior day's activities are completed.

Your first action on Tuesday is to determine why the balance ended so high. Perhaps it was due to an expected cash need that did not occur on Monday. If this were the case, then you would try to ascertain the new date for the funding and adjust your balance accordingly by investing more funds on the next day (Wednesday).

You then might try lowering your balance below the $50,000 level in an attempt to hit the $50,000 figure on average. Since you exceeded it by $20,000 on Tuesday, your goal for Wednesday would be to lower your balance to $30,000, if you can do so without any funding problems. You could choose to reduce the balances gradually over the remainder of the month, but with a big differential, it is probably preferable to catch up faster.

In managing target balances, it is important that the balances be achievable. That is, if they are set too low, based on daily activity, you may never be able to maintain the target without overdrawing the account. This may cause substantial additional charges, so targets should be reviewed for reasonability on a regular basis. The average daily balances should also reflect any adjustments, so that the balances maintained will agree with the adjusted balances that appear on the monthly account analyses.

Figure 7-2: Daily Cash Worksheet					
	Cash Balance Worksheet				
	Our Main Bank				
	Mon.	Tues.	Wed.	Thurs.	Fri.
	06/18/04	06/19/04	06/20/04	06/21/04	06/22/04
Starting Available (Collected) Balance	50,000	70,158	70,158	70,158	70,158
Inflows					
Newark LB deposits	45,578				
Chicago LB deposits	95,210				
Incoming wires/subs	100,000				
Local deposits (OTC)	2,560				
Maturing inv/loan draw	250,150				
TOTAL IN	493,498	0	0	0	0
Outflows					
Contr. disb. funding	198,340				
Direct dep. of payroll	0				
Tax payments	0				
Outgoing wires/subs	0				
Inv made/loans repaid	275,000				
TOTAL OUT	473,340	0	0	0	0
Net Flow	20,158	0	0	0	0
Ending Available Balance	70,158	70,158	70,158	70,158	70,158

Corporate Players

Managing bank relations effectively usually involves gaining a level of control over the interaction between the organization and the bank. This does not mean that all contacts with the bank must come through one person or department, but it does mean that a central oversight group must be aware of operating problems, service needs, or new developments in banking issues critical to the company.

In a decentralized environment or in very large organizations it is impossible for one department to handle all the company's bank dealings and related follow-up. In such cases, many departments and operating locations will have regular contacts with banks. The central (corporate) treasury manager needs to establish a reporting system that keeps him or her informed about what is happening at a local level without threatening local autonomy.

Large organizations with a strong central treasury group and decentralized operating locations regularly schedule meetings to exchange information and share experiences. This interaction can be included as part of another regular financial meeting or it can be a stand-alone meeting. This will depend on how much needs to be discussed. A typical agenda for a regular financial meeting is shown in Figure 7-3 on the next page.

Role playing

As a treasury manager, you may play a role in managing bank relations that is analogous to the role played by your bank counterpart, e.g., your calling officer. Just as your calling officer needs to be fully acquainted with representatives from different product/service areas of the bank, you must know the ins and outs of the company's finances and must learn as much as possible about the company's needs and specific requirements for your banks. This way, you will be able to match up company users of bank services with the providers (e.g., product managers) of that service. In some cases, you will be the user. However, in many cases, especially in larger companies, the users are decentralized.

Internal roles

Organizational influences throughout the company will influence bank relations to a great degree. The degree of centralization or decentralization will determine what role the central corporate treasury manager plays.

For instance, in a very decentralized organization, you will play an internal consulting role, aiding locally autonomous financial managers in developing banking arrangements that satisfy their needs. On the other hand, in a very centralized organization, you will be more involved in identifying banking needs and actually implementing the final arrangements. In either case, you

Figure 7-3: Financial meeting agenda items

Major programs under way
  Consulting studies being conducted
  Changes in bank services
  Changes implemented

Bank performance reviews
  Financial
  Operational report card
  General economic news related to bank
  Discussion of problems

Regulatory update
  Federal Reserve actions
  Congressional actions
  State legislative actions

Organizational issues
  Service needs
  Technology updates
  Staffing changes

Short-term plans
  Possible multi-departmental studies
  New system developments
  Other organizational changes

must monitor the company's cash management system and spectrum of banking services to be effective.

The treasury manager is usually looked upon as the banking expert within the organization. To fulfill this role, you must keep up to date technically. Banks are big helpers in this regard. So are peer groups, such as local or national treasury management associations, but you may actually have more contact with your banking network (taken as a whole) than any other source. The bank group is a valuable resource that should not be ignored.

Corporate Risks

The corporate-bank relationship is really a service relationship. As with any service relationship, there are bound to be risks that may grow over time. These risks include: credit support, bank failure, operational credit risk and disaster recovery.

Credit support

A major risk associated with bank relationships is inadequate credit support—finding out that lines of credit are not available when they are needed. Bank credit has become the source of last resort, so organizations want to feel confident that the lines will be there in case they are needed.

In the past, organizations tested their lines by drawing down on them periodically. This was thought to be a sound test. However, it often was not valid because many of these tests were conducted when the economy was growing, hardly the conditions when the lines would most likely be needed.

The better approach seems to be negotiating a firm revolver for basic financial needs, hoping that other lines, if needed, will be available. It is also possible to arrange for a surplus of lines so that only a portion of them need be available at any one time. In this manner, the organization is not dependent on all its banks when times get tough.

Another important area of bank credit support risk is through the bank's issuance of letters of credit. Standby letters of credit are bank guarantees that substitute the creditworthiness of the bank for that of the original credit seeker. While this is important in the typical business transactions that employ letters of credit, it becomes crucial when standby letters of credit are used to support financial instruments, such as commercial paper.

A number of recent cases have seen commercial paper issuers getting downgraded because of the deteriorating creditworthiness of the guaranteeing financial institution. This has caused many companies to use foreign-owned banks, often Japanese or Swiss, for this type of credit substitution.

Bank failure

The risk of bank failure has been of increasing in concern for treasury managers. The treasury manager should be aware of the limitations of Federal Deposit Insurance Corporation (FDIC) coverage and how possible FDIC actions could affect corporate assets. When banks fail, there are several possible actions that the FDIC can take:

- **Purchase and assumption**
  All deposits, even those beyond the insurance limit (currently $100,000) are purchased by another banking institution.

- **Payoff**
  Depositors are paid (by the FDIC) up to the insured limit. If a depositor has funds above the limit, it must file an insurance claim as a creditor of the failed bank, and it will receive a pro rata share of the liquidation.

- **Transfer**
  Depositors are paid (by another bank) up to the insured limit. Here again, if a depositor has funds above the limit, it must file an insurance claim as a creditor of the failed bank, and it will receive a pro rata share of the liquidation proceeds.

Operational credit risk

The main type of risk associated with cash management services is operational credit risk. This risk is created by timing mismatches in the funds flow into and out of the organization's bank account. This mismatch can be several hours or several days, depending on the transaction.

Since banks provide provisional credit for corporate deposits, the organization faces a risk until the deposited funds are actually collected. If a bank fails while items are in the process of being collected and items are returned, the corporate depositor is at risk for those items.

As far as disbursements are concerned, all checks that were issued but not paid as of the closing of the bank will be returned to the depositor—i.e., the company's suppliers, etc. If the company funded its account in anticipation of clearings that did not occur, the funding would become part of its deposit balance and would be subject to regular FDIC limits.

Disaster recovery considerations

An organization also faces the risk that its bank's computer or communications network will fail to function because of some physical or financial disaster. Most organizations have elaborate system disaster recovery plans, but they often fail to include bank relations as part of the plan.

Earlier, we discussed the risk of credit service failure, but what about cash management services? What are possible courses of action if your collection/concentration network breaks down or its bank balances don't get reported on any given day? You should consider these disasters and determine how to test a disaster plan adequately with the least disruption to normal operating procedures.

Figure 7-4 offers suggestions to consider in formulating a disaster recovery plan. Testing the plan takes considerable planning, time, and effort. Alternative courses of action to the daily

Figure 7-4: Disaster recovery plan checklist for treasury

Is the internal treasury information system included in the organization's overall systems disaster recovery plan?

Are master copies of treasury software in the recovery plan? If not, how can treasury needs be included?

How long will it take to develop a treasury system disaster recovery plan?

Do regular back-up procedures include treasury software and data files?

How often is regular back-up of data? Daily? Within the day?

When was the last time the back-up files were tested for readability, etc.?

How long is required for full system restart?

When was the last time this was tested?

(continued)

Figure 7-4: Disaster recovery plan checklist for treasury (cont.)

If off-the-shelf software (e.g., Microsoft Office) is used, is it the latest version of the program?

When was the last time they were upgraded?

Will new versions read old files?

What are the back-up procedures for treasury hardware?

Is there a back-up PC in the treasury department?

Who is responsible for hardware maintenance?

When was this last performed?

When was the last time that the system's security was reviewed?

Were any changes necessary?

How often are passwords changed?

Is protection from computer viruses available?

How reliable have the telephone lines been?

Does treasury have a separate line for balance reporting?

How often has the line been down during the past year?

What are the back-up plans for a loss in communications?

How portable is the treasury system?

Can it work with a portable laptop computer at another site?

Has this been tested?

Could other staff handle the daily treasury activities in an emergency?

(continued)

Figure 7-4: Disaster recovery plan checklist for treasury (cont.)

Are all the organization's banks located in the same region?

Are they all susceptible to a major power outage or natural disaster?

Should there be back-up banking services (e.g., credit lines or concentration accounts that could be used in an emergency) in another region?

Do all treasury functions have back-up staffing?

If a manager of one of the treasury functions (e.g., short-term investments or foreign exchange) were suddenly unavailable, could his or her responsibilities be handled immediately?

How regularly is formal cross-training conducted?

How long would it take to train new staff?

What impact would the bankruptcy of a major customer have on treasury?

A major vendor?

A major bank?

What has happened in the past if any of these occurred?

routines should be investigated, discussed, and formulated. Then a controlled test should be scheduled, with the cooperation of the organization's banks and treasury management staff.

The test results should be evaluated at a post-mortem meeting. From this evaluation should come any additions, changes or deletions to the recovery plan. Tests should be scheduled at least annually.

Chapter 7 ACTION ITEMS

§ Using Figure 7-1 as a checklist, create a cash management policy document. Keep this document current by documenting changes as they occur.

§ Try to drastically reduce any current target balances maintained at company banks. Investigate all current targets to determine if they have been set based on outdated assumptions (e.g., balances would "always" be at least equal to the target) and can be reduced or eliminated.

§ Adapt Figure 7-2 (typical daily inflows and outflows) to measure variances in key items, using a spreadsheet model. The model should show estimated, actual, and variance figures as of a date. Run the model regularly, such as weekly. Investigate major variances to try to improve the accuracy of the projections.

§ Using Figure 7-3 as a checklist, always have an agenda for any meeting with your banks.

§ Adapt Figure 7-4 to develop your own treasury disaster recovery plan. Document your answers to the checklist, and keep them current.

8

It's Time for a Change

Organizations do not change banks very often because it is a time-consuming process. Thus, unless the bank has not performed at an acceptable level or has been unable or unwilling to provide adequate credit facilities, companies are not likely to move. Past history and the bank's commitment to the company, its industry or lines of business and the community are meaningful signals about the bank's intentions.

Sometimes, however, change is inevitable. For instance, a bank may be too small to keep up with a high-growth company. Mergers, whether between two banks or two companies, can mean change. In addition, change can be created from personal experience. New treasury managers or senior treasury executives may create a change in bank relationships based on their past experience with the organization's current banks or with banks they used somewhere else.

How do you know when it's time for a change in your banking relationships? One way is to periodically evaluate what you are doing and how you have handled change. Figure 8-1 provides a checklist you can use in reviewing your current treasury practices. How you respond to the items will determine further actions.

Making changes to an existing network is never easy. This evaluative approach can help you identify what needs attention and what does not.

Figure 8-1: Evaluating Your Current Banking Structure

- *Establish a bank monitoring system to alert you to changes, out-of-the-ordinary situations, and problems.*
  It should be an exception reporting system that measures such things as the effectiveness of your collection system, the cost-effectiveness of the concentration system, the efficient use of controlled disbursements, and the accurate and acceptable levels of bank service charges.

- *Conduct a major review every four or five years to evaluate the system.*
  Do one sooner if there has been a significant change in the company, such as a merger, divestiture, or major expansion in business lines.

- *Review documentation for all major activities as they are now being done.*
  If there is no documentation, this is your starting point. Use this as a first step in determining how detailed a review is warranted. Recreating documentation, while possibly time-consuming, is a valuable exercise.

- *Determine when the last change to the system was made.*
  If there have been organizational or other changes within the last two years that resulted in new banks or bank services, consider doing a full review aimed at incorporating any new operations.

(continued)

132

Figure 8-1: Evaluating Your Current Banking Structure
(cont.)

- *Determine when collection points, disbursement float, cash concentration, and bank compensation levels were last reviewed.*
  This should be done whenever a major event has occurred or every five years, whichever is sooner.

- *Review the last major problem that occurred, or the last few if there have been several during the past 12-18 months.*
  This is another symptom of a system in need of change. If too many problems occur, it could signal that you are dealing with the wrong banks or that you have some basic impediment in your system.

- *Do a regular bank review at least annually or whenever there has been a major change.*

- *Review charges and rates for uncollected overdrafts.*
  Make sure that the overdraft was caused by the company and not the bank. If the latter, get the charges waived.

- *Calculate a float factor for each deposit account monthly.*
  To do this, calculate average daily deposits by dividing the number of calendar days in the month into the total dollar deposits for the month. Be careful to get all of the deposits, since the calendar month may be longer than the applicable accounting period (many firms use 30 days as their normal accounting period). Next, find the float figure from your account analysis that matches the deposit account, and divide it by the daily deposit figure. This gives you the number of calendar days that it took for deposits to clear.

(continued)

Figure 8-1: Evaluating Your Current Banking Structure
(continued)

The formula is:

Float Factor = [Avg. Daily Float] / [Total Deposits/No. of Days in Month]

Note that the float factor does not include mail or processing float—i.e., delays created by the postal system or at the point of deposit. These float figures are determined by conducting a full collection study. You are looking for consistency (or lack thereof) over time. Lockbox accounts should be near 1.4. (Remember 1 business day = 1.4 calendar days.) Over the counter deposit accounts may vary, but if they are for local check deposits, they also should be near the 1.4 mark.

- *Research wide swings or numbers that do not make sense by checking the deposit figures and/or having the bank verify the float figure.*

- *Finally, just ask yourself—does anything just not make sense?*
Take a step back and look at your system.

As part of your review, you should establish an action plan for implementing change. The first step is to categorize the type of action into one of the following:

- **Simple fixes**
It should be relatively easy to reduce or eliminate idle balances, eliminate dormant accounts, and reduce unneeded charges. These are actions that you can do quickly.

- **Judgment calls**
  If you wish to replace services or revise banking arrangements by consolidating services or by replacing costly services with more economical ones, it will take some time to decide on an approach. It will take additional time to complete the activity required to fix the problem.

- **Longer-term projects**
  You may determine that you will have to review overall banking needs, revise treasury information systems, undertake an RFP for all banking services, or study whether to centralize/decentralize banking services. These are full-blown projects and will require time and resources to complete.

Next, determine the resources required for making changes, in terms of staff time (including your time), new software, bank services, new hardware, and any outside support (treasury consultants, etc.).

Using RFPs Wisely

RFPs have changed the way bank services are selected. More and more, companies have incorporated the RFP process into their selection procedures. Figure 8-2, taken from the 2002-2003 Phoenix-Hecht Blue Book of Bank Prices shows how larger companies and upper middle market companies handle service selection. The results show behavior in 2000 and in 2002.

The figure shows distinct differences in the practices of different-sized companies. For example, larger firms are more likely to request competitive bids (i.e., use RFPs), negotiate price guarantees for a fixed period of time, and review charges annually. Companies in the upper middle category (but still bigger than most middle market firms) are more likely to stay with existing banks for new services. Neither group admits to using price as a serious decision factor, although I have never seen a survey that found that price was as significant as experience tells us it is.

Figure 8-2: Buyer Behavior				
	2000		**2002**	
Statement	**Large Corp.**	**Upper Mid**	**Large Corp.**	**Upper Mid**
Request competitive bids on new cash management services	67%	50%	64%	46%
Buy new services only from existing banks	62%	73%	62%	73%
Cash management services won by lower prices	29%	20%	22%	20%
Company has changed banks because of price increases	12%	9%	13%	10%
Company negotiates price guarantees for specific periods of time	66%	45%	67%	50%
Company annually reviews bank prices	71%	56%	65%	58%

Source: *Phoenix-Hecht Blue Book of Bank Prices*, 2002-2003 edition

Why use RFPs?

The main purpose in using an RFP is to formalize the service selection process. Even if you don't want to use a formal RFP, you can still learn from the RFP process. That is, using some of the methodology will enable you to make a better decision.

The RFP process is a standardized approach to selecting bank services. It offers more objective, documented, and informed decisions. In addition, it gives you better control over the timing and implementation of bank services. In today's business world of smaller staffs and limited time, RFPs offer a ray of hope.

Many major service banks receive a substantial number of RFPs annually. This creates a great deal of work for both the company and the bank, but it does not seem to show any signs of abating (as suggested by Figure 8-2). I believe there are a number of reasons for increased RFP activity:

- **Need to reduce operating costs**
  This is probably the most important reason. RFPs are

useful because, if done properly, they instill competition among service providers, which usually translates into lower prices.

- **Advances in new technology for existing services**
  Competitors must be "creative" to get the business. This usually means that they will offer the latest state-of-the-art service.

- **How companies view non-credit services**
  More and more, cash managers regard their core cash management services as commodity-type services. This means that several providers can be expected to offer acceptable services. The RFP process assures an objective and optimal selection.

- **Significant unbundling of non-credit service pricing**
  It is often difficult to understand how much services will cost because each provider has a different array of service charges. Using an RFP forces the providers to translate pricing to a common denominator.

- **Bank mergers and acquisitions**
  These activities create uncertainty for cash managers as the new banks that emerge may not be recognizable to the cash manager. RFPs can help you understand what the new bank has to offer and how interested it is in the company's business.

Ready-made questionnaires

The bank selection process has become more of a science than an art. Treasury managers have books available for their use that contain questionnaires that have been prepared by experts. The two main books are:

- *How to Prepare an RFP for Treasury Services* (Third edition), by Kenneth L. Parkinson and Raymond P. Ruzek, available at www.tisconsulting.com

- *Standardized RFPs*, by the Association for Financial Professional (two volumes: domestic and global), available at www.afponline.org

You can use these questionnaires to obtain more detail on new services. Using the questionnaires that are appropriate for your service needs and editing them so that only the questions that apply to your situation are used, you can compare responses from several banks. It is important to use just the questions that you need, or else you will end up confusing the banks and making it harder for them to respond in a timely fashion.

This process can help narrow the field before final selection. Before selecting the finalists, you can meet and even visit each bank before choosing the bank to provide the desired service.

In making a final decision for a non-credit service, there is never a real concern that the bank will not be able to supply the service. With credit services, this is not always so. For instance, a bank may not be able to nor want to supply all the credit facility itself. In these cases, it can put together a loan syndicate or take direction from the customer. The bank's experience doing this and the customer's past experience with the bank on credit facilities are important factors in making the final decision.

In making a decision for credit or non-credit services, two other attributes are relevant. One is the assurance that the bank is large enough and sophisticated enough to grow with the company. The other is whether the bank is knowledgeable about the company's main lines of business. This is important so the bank can help the company in dealing with situations that are specific to its industrial lines. Banks without this special expertise may be of limited help to the company.

The RFP Process

Preparing RFPs does not have to be a time-consuming task. However, time spent on the front end (i.e., before soliciting bids) will expedite the decision-making process. You should devote adequate time to defining the problem or describing the desired service in detail. If information on the service needs is required, it should be collected well before the RFPs go out.

Exhibit 8-3 shows the standard items that should be included in any RFP. The RFP process is usually a two-step decision-making procedure. The responses to the RFP are compared, usually in a master matrix. One approach uses weightings to value each response, similar to the report card concept show in chapter 6.

Exhibit 8-3: Standard RFP Items

Contact(s) from your organization

Current system: volumes, procedures, services used

New system: New services desired and changes to current system contemplated

Detailed questionnaires for each type of service

Decision timetable

Step one

Preparing for responses entails setting up a decision matrix to evaluate answers. To do this, assign a weight to each question (use a 1-3 scale, with 3 being the most important). You will also score each bank's response (use a 1-5 scale, with 5 being highest). Multiplying the weight by the score and adding up the products for each section provide you with a quantitative rating for each bank, section by section. You should also ask enough open-ended questions to obtain a qualitative impression for each service for each bank. These open-ended questions should be customized to fit your needs.

After the responses are received, score each bank. It usually is more effective to do this by section or service, but this is not mandatory. It should be easy to determine what the best and worst responses are and to judge whether other responses are closer to the best or the worst. Also, you must read the answers to the free-form, qualitative questions. You may want to assign them a score, too, just to remind yourself which banks provided good or poor answers.

Don't expect to be satisfied with all the answers as they originally appear in the proposals. You may have to ask a bank to
clarify its answer or provide additional information.

I find that making the first cut in narrowing down a field of
several banks usually seems to happen by itself. As you review
the proposals, you will find that the responders fall into two
groups: banks that look as if they can meet your needs and banks
that are not a good match for your company. Sometimes there is a
third group of banks—those that excel on one or two services but
are not as good overall. If you are willing to divide your non-
credit business among two or three banks, you may wish to keep
these banks in contention.

Step two

It is not unusual to have second and third rounds of follow- up
questions for the banks making the first cut. If more than three
banks made the first cut, you will need another evaluation to narrow the finalists to no more than three banks. You may also ask finalists to make presentations, or you may want to visit the banks.

This is the point where references are checked. If the references don't seem comparable to your situation, ask for additional
ones or check with your professional cash management network
(e.g., other members of your local association or industry trade
group). Evaluate the feedback—are you satisfied?

Finally, make your final decision. Talk to the winner first
and agree on a timetable right at the start. Notify the other RFP
responders RIGHT AWAY! Tell them why they were not selected.
Remember: you may want to deal with them in the future.

Ethical Considerations

Corporate treasury managers who spend all their time looking for
loss leaders will end up paying in the end. While bankers do not
trade pricing information or other "private" secrets, the reputation of a treasury manager and his or her way of doing business
becomes well known quickly among the small society of bankers.
Banks will not continue to offer attractive pricing or innovative
services if they get nothing in return. Taking this approach would
also seem to violate the company's bank policy to obtain reasonably priced services.

Taking advantage of inefficiencies is another unethical activity that has occurred in the past. A good example of this was the E. F. Hutton incident, in which the company took advantage of smaller banks' inability to determine whether a balance was good or not. As a result, the company's local branch managers were able to create "phantom" deposits to inflate their sales figures. In this instance, their cash management system provided financial benefits by providing the mechanism—funds concentration reporting—that the local managers used. Eventually, the phony system was detected, and the company was punished severely.

It is not uncommon for treasury managers to deal with smaller, less sophisticated banks that do not have the same resources or offer the same degree of technical currency as the large cash management banks. This does not mean that companies should take advantage of this situation by moving funds too soon or undercompensating the bank. All banks should be treated as equally and fairly as possible.

Some organizations try to use bank officers to spy on other company operating units or on competitors. For instance, in heavily decentralized situations, a central treasury manager may attempt to use the banker to gather intelligence on other units. This almost never helps the bank relationship. Treasury managers who attempt to use bankers in this way should reevaluate this practice. A bank calling officer should not be used as a replacement for internal communication and cooperation.

Finally, misusing the RFP process raises ethical considerations. For instance, consulting with a banker to compose an RFP package gives that banker considerably more information and influence over the proposals that will be submitted. I question whether treasury managers who do this really need to go through the RFP process at all. Other bidding banks usually can recognize when another bank has had a hand in writing the RFP, so they are not likely to give their best bid for the business. Maintaining a level playing field for all banks gives you the best chance of receiving honest, objective proposals.

Chapter 8 ACTION ITEMS

§ Using Figure 8-1 as a checklist, evaluate your current banking structure. After first doing such an evaluation, maintain current responses to the checklist items by periodically reviewing the items. This should be done at least annually.

§ One item shown in Figure 8-1—-calculating float factors—-may be more effective if done monthly for each depository account. Float factors, which measure how long it has taken for deposited checks to be made available, are simple to compute and can be easily compared over time and against standards. The usual standard is 1.40, which represents one business day; i.e., the goal is to clear everything overnight (meaning the same thing as one business day).

§ Maintain an RFP *diary* to record and be able to analyze how effective the RFP process was for each RFP project. Record timetables, including which deadlines were not met and why they were not met, missing volumes, common bank problems or misunderstandings, special problems or developments of note, and overall satisfaction level with the project.

§ Set up a spreadsheet model to compute a decision matrix for use in any RFP project. Cut and paste in questions from RFP questionnaires, assign weights to each question, enter the simple formula to compute each score, and summarize each service questionnaire by bank.

9

The Old Standby—Credit Services

Let's not forget about credit, in its various forms. It still is the backbone of many companies' financial strength, regardless of whether they borrow directly from banks or indirectly through the money market (e.g., via commercial paper) backed up by bank lines of credit.

For many years, commercial banks were the providers of short-term finance and credit services to corporations. In recent years, however, they have lost their role as providers of short-term financing for larger corporations to the commercial paper market. The amount of commercial paper outstanding now easily exceeds the total commercial and industrial loans made by banks to corporations.

Banks still support the commercial paper market through the provision of backup credit facilities and other short-term, stop-gap forms of financing. They have faced further competition in the smaller corporate market from non-bank sources (e.g., commercial finance companies). Banks, however, remain a popular source for short-term funds for many companies, even if in a smaller role.

Types of Credit Services

Banks offer a variety of credit services. Your choices will depend on your organization's size, creditworthiness, and structure. Banks are sensitive to the organization's structure and are wary of lending to holding companies because there is little substance at the holding company level. The products or services of value are produced by subsidiaries.

Credit services can be classified as either *facility-oriented* or *transaction-oriented*. Examples of both types of credit services are shown in Figure 9-1. Facility-oriented services have limits established for their activities. The simplest example is a regular line of credit. With this service, the bank sets a credit limit for the borrower to draw against, subject to the bank's approval and availability of funds. The borrower cannot exceed the credit line limit set by the bank.

Facility-oriented credit services

Facility-based services are often considered as part of the base relationship between bank and corporation. They are also commonly negotiated for longer periods of time (e.g., years), especially in the case of credit lines, revolvers, and term loans.

Regular lines

As the figure shows, there are several forms of credit lines that are typical facility-oriented services. The most common is a *regular line of credit*, which is usually negotiated and in effect for 364 days, renewable annually unless something serious has occurred that changes the borrower's financial position.

This type of line is generally unsecured, with the rate set at the bank's prime rate or the London Interbank Offered Rate (LIBOR) plus a spread. The spread over LIBOR depends on the borrower's creditworthiness, with stronger credits receiving narrower spreads than weaker credits. Weaker credits may also be charged a spread over prime.

The borrower compensates the bank for the line by paying a commitment fee, usually priced as a fraction of one per cent of the line of credit. Stronger credits pay a lower fee, such as ½% or lower, while weaker credits pay higher rates. Also, the commitment fee may be assessed against the full line or just the outstand-

Figure 9-1: Types of Credit Services

Facility-oriented services

- Regular lines (unsecured)
- Pre-signed (grid) notes
- Backup lines
- Revolving credit agreements (revolvers)
- Term loans
- Letters of credit (standby)

Transaction-oriented services

- House lines (FX, daylight overdrafts, etc.)
- Uncommitted lines of credit
- Letters of credit (commercial)
- Bankers acceptances
- Commercial paper (sales)
- Credit enhancement (for commercial paper)
- Loan participations
- Private placements and other investment banking services
- Trade/project financing
- Merger and acquisition assistance/financing
- Advisory services and merchant banking

ing portion of the line not being used, depending on the negotiations between borrower and lender.

Borrowers can tap regular lines as they need funds. If the LIBOR pricing option is selected, there is usually a delay in the availability of funds ranging from one to three business days, depending on the borrower's size and financial strength. Borrowing at prime is usually possible on the same day. Borrowing under these lines is usually for a fixed period of time, but most loans are prepayable without penalty.

When you borrow in the U.S. for short-term needs, you must sign a promissory note and deliver this to your bank. To facilitate borrowing, many organizations pre-sign a note for the full amount of the line. This allows them to draw down on the line daily and repay as needed without generating new notes for the borrowings. Such arrangements are sometimes referred to as *grid notes* because the bank keeps track of your borrowings and repayments in a grid format.

CP backup lines

Although many large organizations tap the commercial paper (CP) market for their short-term working capital funding, they usually are required to maintain backup lines of credit to cover the CP program when they initiate it. To obtain a satisfactory short-term credit rating and to maintain it after the program has been launched, you must maintain these lines. The major rating agencies (e.g., Standard & Poor's, Moody's, and Fitch) require CP borrowers to confirm that the lines are in place.

These lines must be committed lines of credit or a stronger form, such as a revolving credit agreement. It is important to note the distinction between backup and guarantee. These lines back up outstanding CP, but the borrower is not legally required to use them to pay off maturing CP issues.

Revolving credit agreement

When an organization wants the strongest form of bank credit facility, it negotiates a *revolving credit agreement*. A revolver has many of the same features as a committed line—e.g., borrowing at prime to LIBOR plus a spread, a commitment fee, no prepayment penalties, and a notification period. Revolvers are often for larger amounts of credit than regular credit lines, and they are typically in effect for longer than one year. In many cases, more than one bank participates in the facility, acting as a bank syndicate.

If there are multiple banks involved, you usually select one bank to be the lead, or *agent*, bank. The agent bank acts on behalf of the other banks in negotiating the terms of the loan facility with you and is paid extra for this. The agent bank can pull the syndicate together for you, or you can negotiate with each participating bank as to the amount and compensation.

Some treasury managers negotiate all aspects of their revolvers with the syndicated banks individually, but it makes sense to tap an agent bank—probably your main bank—and let the agent negotiate for all members of the syndicate. The agent bank also supplies legal services to sign off on the agreement before the revolver takes effect. In the end a revolver is a binding legal document. You are expected to pay all the legal fees and an additional facility fee for establishing the revolver.

Some revolvers are set up for specific purposes, such as to provide financial backing for a merger situation. Weaker credits can also negotiate a revolver, but the final credit facility may be secured by a lien on the borrower's assets.

If borrowers are planning to consolidate some of their short-term borrowing and convert these loans to a medium-term loan or if they wish to finance an asset over multiple years, they often negotiate a *term loan option* with their revolver. Term loans can be negotiated independently as well. A term loan is simply a fixed-rate loan for 2-10 years. Rates are usually fixed, and you amortize the loan by repaying it over the life of the borrowing.

Standby letters of credit are bank guarantees that are triggered when an event occurs, such as the borrower needing to show that it has financial backing. House lines can be complex in that their limit may only be established internally by the bank without informing the company officially.

Transaction-Oriented Credit Services

Transaction-oriented services, on the other hand, are stand-alone services. Banks add a fee or build in another form of compensation into the price of the transaction. Treasury managers usually shop around to compare prices and service features for most transaction-oriented credit services.

Uncommitted lines are shown as transaction-oriented services because you are not required to pay explicitly for the service. Banks set house lines to limit their risk for any single customer for special financial transactions, such as trading in foreign exchange.

Uncommitted lines

An *uncommitted line of credit* is a line that a bank offers at a point in time to a potential borrower without any other compensation other than interest for a period of time. Such loans may not be rolled over at maturity like other bank loans because the bank is not committed to continuing the line on an ongoing basis, nor will the bank confirm that there is an uncommitted facility in place as part of your financial audit review. This makes such lines unreliable. You should treat uncommitted line offers as windfalls if they provide a cheap loan at a particular time. Think of this type of line as a facility to do credit business with the bank.

A *commercial letter of credit* is used to provide financial coverage of specific trade transactions (hence the name, commercial). Commercial letters of credit provide financing for imports and exports, which typically have longer transaction periods than routine domestic (U.S.) transactions. Treasury managers look for the most economical form of financing imports and exports, so they have little "brand loyalty" with commercial letters of credit. Many treasury managers keep up-to-date lists of bank prices for commercial letters of credit by geographic region, often tapping the cheapest provider.

I have included *bankers' acceptances* (BAs) as a transaction-oriented credit service. Although we usually think of BAs as money market securities, these facilities are arranged through the bank that issues a commercial letter of credit for transactions such as imports or exports.

Some of the larger banks also provide commercial paper sales and support for borrowers wishing to tap the CP market. The bank acts as a CP dealer and receives a fee for its services. Often, this service is for CP issuers with lower than the top credit ratings.

In addition, many banks support CP sales for weaker credit or other organizations that would not be able to issue CP in their own right. This is called *credit enhancement* and consists of a bank standby letter of credit for the full amount of the CP program, which guarantees all CP issued and transfers the credit risk to the underwriting bank instead of the issuer. The CP could be issued by any other institution or the guaranteeing bank itself.

The remaining items in the list shown in Figure 9-1—*loan participations, merger and acquisition financing, private placements* (of debt) and *other investment banking services, trade/project financing,* and *advisory services*— represent special financial services that banks offer to provide financing for special purposes. Banks are compensated either by direct fee payment or by a fee built into the transaction.

Although price alone may not be the deciding factor, there is value in thorough comparison shopping. Sometimes the willingness of the bank to finance the transaction at all may be the deciding factor. With other types of transaction-oriented services, such as advisory or consulting assistance, you may find that your selection is somewhat limited as all banks may not offer all these services.

Negotiating Credit Services

Since transaction-oriented services generally have their prices built into the final rate, they do not require the same level of negotiation. On the other hand, establishing facility-oriented credit services can be involved because you must negotiate with your banks to obtain the best facilities for your organization. Like most financial activities, it pays to be prepared when you negotiate credit services.

A useful tool for negotiating credit services, such as an uncommitted line of credit or revolving credit agreement, is a *term sheet*. A term sheet is simply a list of items that you wish to negotiate with your bankers.

Creating Your Term Sheet

Typical items to consider on your term sheet are shown in Figure 9-2. While all items may not apply to your individual case, they offer a good list of points to consider before you begin your negotiations.

You may be more concerned with getting the best terms for some of the items shown and not as concerned for others. If this is the case, annotate your term sheet appropriately.

Once you have reviewed the items shown in Figure 9-2 and edited the list for your use, you are ready for negotiations. You may want to have different term sheets depending on the type of service you are negotiating or the type or size of the financial institution with which you are negotiating.

Expect to have to give and take, as is the case with any good negotiation. This is where your work on your term sheet can pay

Figure 9-2: Term Sheet Items

Secured or unsecured? What type of collateral available (if secured)?

Rate options: Prime? + or - ? LIBOR ? + spread? Are other money market rates possible?

What is the rate-setting mechanism—i.e., exactly how is borrowing rate computed?

Number of days to use for interest calculation (360? 365/366?). It is appropriate to use 365/366 for bank loans.

Compensation arrangements: Commitment fee on used or unused amounts? Facility fee for revolver (i.e., upfront charge)?

Length of time credit facility will be in effect? How renewable?

Timing notifications or delays in takedowns? Do these differ by base rate chosen?

Covenants required? How negotiable?

Any other processing costs, etc.

off. If you have marked the items that are more important to you, you will know which ones you have to hold out on and which items you can give in on.

Credit services can play an integral role if your organization depends on external financing to function smoothly in its operations. You may not think you need to spend much time in developing a strategic approach to procuring financial services, but this would be a mistake. Considering the extent of the services listed in Figure 9-1, you should have an appreciation for the opportunities that exist for handling the financial needs for your organization. Banks today offer far more than lines of credit, as the scope of the services discussed above indicates.

Depending on your circumstances, you may need more support from your banks in credit facilities than in non-credit services. This is something you have to decide because it affects how you approach the banks and what you can offer. If you need more in credit, then you can offer your cash management services as part of your negotiating package to make your organization look more attractive.

Chapter 9 ACTION ITEMS

§ Create an inventory of credit services, using Figure 9-1 as a guide. Maintain an active list of those services currently used or recently used. Refer to the figure as needed in planning the company's credit service needs.

§ Detail, using a spreadsheet model, the features of each line of credit, including the following items:
  • Amount of the line
  • Time period line is in effect
  • Commitment fee and any other compensation (indicate whether fee is on full amount of line or just on unused amount)
  • Formula for computing interest rate (e.g., LIBOR + 25 basis points)

Chapter 9 ACTION ITEMS (cont.)

§ Log and track short-term borrowings, using a spreadsheet model and including the following data items:
  • Bank name
  • Total line available
  • Amount of loan
  • Interest rate
  • Repayments

§ Maintain a current list of credit banks, showing amounts, compensation, etc. for each bank. Keep this as up-to-date as possible, using a spreadsheet model.

§ Do a cost comparison for letters of credit, showing which banks are more economical for type of letter of credit, country involved, or any other decision criteria applicable to your company.

§ For special financings, such as merger and acquisition financing, private placements, or trade/project financing, maintain a log of which banks responded competitively in the past for use in making future decisions.

§ Develop your own standard term sheet, using Figure 9-2 as a checklist. Use this sheet to prepare for negotiations for credit facilities.

10

Get Ready for an Interesting Ride

What is going to shape banking services and relations in the short-term and longer-term future? How should you prepare? How difficult will it be to optimize banking services in the new business landscape? Will banks change their attitudes toward offering non-credit and credit services?

There is no doubt that the financial world is changing. In the forefront are improved communications and processing technologies that will make current products and services obsolete and enable organizations to take advantage of a more efficient electronic environment. The continuing growth in national banking will bring customers benefits—such as wider geographic coverage and better concentration of collections—as well as drawbacks—such as fewer suppliers of services and reduced competition or increased pressure from banks for additional business to offset low returns from less profitable products and services.

Shifting to a More Electronic World

It has taken a long time, but in recent years, check volumes in the U.S. have finally shown sharp declines. Does this mean that we will finally realize the "checkless" society envisioned more than 30 years ago? Probably not for a while, but technology combined with enabling legislation and customer desire for more efficient services should have a significant impact on corporate bank relations.

First of all, banks will have to adapt to the new rules that will be in effect. Banks still obtain a great deal of revenue from check-based services and need to be able to broaden their product and service lines to encompass expanded electronic processing. Organizations will also have to give up their use of checks. They and their trading partners will have to negotiate new payment methods, timing, delivery, and payment forms.

Newer methods for transferring information will play significant roles in the changeover from paper-based systems. The Internet, more specifically, the World Wide Web (or just the Web), has proven to be invaluable in helping change the way we look at payments and related information. Imaging technology has also enabled companies to "see" documents in minutes and hours, instead of days and possibly weeks.

The culmination of all this technology should be enhanced electronic payments, faster data delivery, less emphasis on check float, and simplified bank service needs.

The Web

The Web has changed how we think about things. It was not too long ago that e-mail was just an experiment and the Web was a network of just a few "techie" users. All this has changed, of course, and the Web shows no sign of slowing down and has fast become a part of everyday business life.

The Web helps with bank relations by improving banker-customer communications and by simplifying the reporting of bank account information. E-mail provides customers and bankers with an efficient, around-the-clock method of communication. This should make it easier for banks and their customers to interact whenever necessary, such as researching errors or following up on a change in services. Customers should experience faster turnaround time and fewer games of telephone tag.

Most banks have shifted to the Web to provide a cost-beneficial means of delivering information. Using the Web reduces the costs of making changes to bank information services because the software for communicating with and accessing information from the bank does not have to be distributed to each user to load on local PCs. Also, by using the Web as an interface, the bank can develop additional services to deliver more information, such as copies of checks paid or checks received or positive pay exception items that need final resolution.

The Web can provide much information about your existing banking activities as well as information about new banking and financial services offered by your banks and other competing institutions. With widespread availability of high-speed, broadband connections with the Internet, treasury managers can take better advantage of the Web's resources to learn about new services, look up historical data, or stay up to date on stories in the financial press. Many resources are free on the Web; others require a subscription fee.

If you are still using the Internet primarily for e-mail and accessing your bank information reports, you have not begun to tap its overall potential. Banking and business sites are plentiful on the Web. Most of them are specific to an organization, such as a bank or corporation or governmental unit, while others reflect the combined efforts of members of a trade association or industry-related task force. It is interesting to group sites by type. Figure 10-1 shows categories of Web sites that are useful for treasury managers.

Figure 10-1: Types of Useful Web Sites

Bank sites

Non-bank financial sites

Link sites

Government sites

Association sites

Publication sites

Commercial and investment banks around the world offer sites, many of which feature descriptive material on wholesale and retail bank products and services. You can search through bank sites for more information about services or for updates on industry issues. Most sites are simply the bank's name followed by *.com*.

Bank sites also contain private links for customers to retrieve account and transaction information, move funds, and download other data. Some banks also offer electronic bill presentation and payment services, acting as consolidators for sellers that do not have their own electronic payment capability. Use of Web-based payment services by consumers has been growing steadily and should become a common way for consumers to pay bills instead of using checks.

Banks are not the only financial institutions that have adopted the Web. *Non-bank financial firms* that have useful Web sites include investment banks, finance companies, public accounting firms, financial consulting firms (many are spin-offs from the public accounting firms), financial research firms, and financial industry trade groups. These sites offer service descriptions, research information and statistics, position papers on current topics, explanatory features on strategic issues, and copies of articles published by members of the firms.

Link sites function as hubs, providing hot links to many other sites, usually with a short description. Two of the best are the Treasury Management Pages and Phoenix-Hecht. Both sites have a large number of links organized by topic, such as information on interest rates, references for books or other financial publications. Also included with this group are general information sites like Yahoo. Many of the sites noted in other groups have links pages that are similar to this group.

Government sites are excellent sources for statistics and other government publications, such as tax forms. The Federal Reserve and the Federal government (e.g., SEC's EDGAR) are heavy users and providers of information over the Web. Most government documents that are available to the public are accessible over the Web. These sites can be valuable resources for research projects.

Trade association sites offer descriptions of their member services, publications, educational programs, and links to industry-related locations. The treasury, credit, accounting, supply chain (purchasing), risk and insurance, banking, and automated clearing house associations are all well represented on the Web. Most association sites have special private links for members that include access to special reports, such as survey results, or proprietary data, such as investment benchmarks or industry financial indicators.

Many *trade publications*—financial and otherwise—offer informative Web sites. Some, such as the *Wall Street Journal, International Treasurer, American Banker, Institutional Investor*, and *Euromoney*, charge for the full service but offer some items for free. Others, such as *Treasury and Risk Management* magazine, *Global Treasury News*, and *Business and Finance* magazine offer access free with or without a registration procedure. These sites can help keep you up-to-date on general financial issues and events as well as specific banking topics.

Overall, the Web has added many rich resources that can help you do a better job. You can stay informed, look up past data, review the types of services banks are offering, and keep abreast of the financial markets.

Imaging

Improved technology for automatic data capture is the latest step in improved communications services offered by banks to their customers. Over time, technology has moved from simple photocopying to optical scanning to digital imaging and from mailing copies of remittances to transmitting images of the actual documents electronically. The latest technology involves the digitizing of paper into an electronic copy of the original.

Imaging has changed the way that banks deliver information to their customers and substantially reduced the time it takes for customers to receive the information. For treasury managers, this means faster turnaround of vital information about checks cleared, checks received via a lockbox, or checks that could be forged—i.e., those items flagged by positive pay filters. Imaging eliminates the need for costly rapid movement of paper documentation regarding payments and receipts.

The use of images of paper-based payment items (i.e., checks and remittance documents) helps pave the way for increased use of electronic payment methods. If images can move much faster than paper, it stands to reason that paper-based float will likely be substantially reduced. In addition, by capturing images closer to the point of payment, whether at a retail counter or sent from a company location to a local postal service branch, mail and processing float can also be substantially reduced.

Will this be enough to trigger wholesale scrapping of checks for electronic methods of payment? More time is needed to answer this question, but for now image capture and related services are big steps in that direction.

Imaging can also be used internally to transmit internal financial information from one location to another, such as with credit granting procedures and analysis, copies of payment transaction data, or for instructions in setting up accounts or documenting financial transactions. Images of transaction documentation can be conveniently attached to e-mails in response to inquiries from other employees or vendors.

More electronic payments on the way

As reports of decreased check volume continue, growth in electronic payments should not be too surprising. It is becoming much easier to handle and create electronic payments, and these types of transactions have much lower costs associated with them than paper-based transactions.

There are no paper reconciliation services to purchase, and storage of past transactions is fully electronic, not requiring massive storage space. Paying electronically, including on-line via the Web, has become more accepted and is growing in use at both the consumer end and the business customer end.

For a long time, growth in electronic payments came mainly from direct deposit applications, such as payroll, dividends, and pension payments. Direct debit growth has been relatively slow since many customers did not want to cede control to the seller, especially with payments between businesses.

There now seems to be growing acceptance of electronic payments, spurred on by the growth of e-commerce Web sites and use of the Web for making payments. For consumer payments, the shift was relatively easy, substituting plastic (debit cards, credit cards) for checks. Retailers at the point of sale/purchase also have made making electronic payments easier by taking plastic and e-checks, which essentially convert paper checks to ACH debits (like a debit card) at the point of sale.

Companies engaged in industries where electronic payments are growing will have greater needs for merchant processing services for credit and debit card business provided by their banks. Many companies now include such services in their bank service selection process (e.g., by RFP).

Bank lockbox departments are even being called upon by their customers to accept and process credit and debit card transactions that are mixed in with check payments. This is a long way from simple opening of envelopes and making a copy of the check. It is a convenient way to merge all customer payments into one source and to transmit data about all types of payments received.

E-commerce and EDI effects

E-commerce and electronic data interchange (EDI) hold the potential for substantial growth in electronic payments. During the rise of the *dot-coms*, it looked as if e-commerce would be the vehicle these firms used to expand their business. In addition, because it was an electronic medium, these firms were more likely to assume that payments would be made electronically.

The fall of the dot-coms hurt this development, but the spotlight on the Internet brought by the dot-coms undoubtedly helped convince more established firms to consider the Web as an alternative sales track. This is the good news, because it means that these firms will see growth in electronic payments and will probably rethink how they use paper vs. electronic for other payments as well. Also, these organizations, as they have done in the past, are likely to turn to their bankers for help and additional services to handle this new type of payment option.

Many banks have been willing partners with industry task forces or volunteer groups that have developed standardized methods and systems for ordering, processing, billing, and paying for purchases electronically. Much of this was previously done through EDI, but later development went beyond EDI to include payments made in e-commerce transactions made via the Web.

E-commerce applications range from simple *bill pay* to more sophisticated *e-procurement*. Banks have helped customers develop electronic payment capabilities by offering processing, consolidation, and payment services. Banks have also helped their customers prepare to make and accept electronic payments.

E-commerce and EDI alone might not have been sufficient to fuel a steady growth in electronic payments. In fact, most of the focus has shifted from EDI to e-commerce due to the latter's flexibility and wider scope. When added to an environment of low interest rates (hence, low value for payment float), increased costs associated with check processing, and a recognition by treasury managers that electric payments might help reduce exposure to fraud, e-commerce developments can provide the mechanism to streamline payments and handle the growth in payment transactions resulting from on-line purchases by consumers and businesses.

Changes in the Banking World

The banking world is not standing still, either. Banks have tapped into new technologies to offer more comprehensive services to their customers. They have also shifted their focus from a traditional customer-bank relationship based on borrowing and sizable account balances to a streamlined, fee-driven relationship.

Banks have also reassessed many of their traditional products and services to decide whether to invest more in technology to improve an older service or to eliminate it altogether. They have reevaluated their returns on solitary credit facilities, which have been set up by companies as low cost financial insurance or safety lines. They also have had to decide how they will participate in the development of national banking in the U.S. Some will choose to grow and compete with the large multi-state banks while others will stay small and local or agree to merge with one of the leaders in the national banking movement.

National banking and bank consolidation

Corporations and banks have been working together for years, and there is no reason to believe that their relationships won't continue. The heavy level of competition for large corporate customers has proved beneficial to the corporate treasury manager, the buyer of those services.

As the number of banks diminishes and a relative handful of banks evolve into controlling the market for cash management services, it may not be as easy for treasury managers to use competitive bidding as judiciously as in the past. This does not mean that the sellers of the services will be able to raise prices substantially because it may create enough perceived opportunity for other potential service providers.

Also, with the growth of very large banks, there has been a growth of much smaller, regional (if not local) banks that can offer "plain vanilla" cash management services that are perfectly acceptable to local smaller firms and even to some larger firms looking for simple processing at a reasonable charge.

Banks that do not do a thorough job of identifying and controlling their costs will face problems in the future. Their customers have become better educated, in many instances because of knowledge gained from their banks. With these educated consumers, however, have come experienced users and purchasers of services - today's corporate treasury managers. This means that the banks will have to apply more resources to maintaining their market share and will find new business harder to come by.

Bank consolidation is becoming a fact of life in the U.S. As a large part of corporate-bank relations involves the interaction of bank and corporate staffs, mega-mergers between large regional and money center banks will significantly affect corporate-bank relations. The successful mergers will be those that preserve existing personal relationships and build on them.

Consolidation has another possible effect on bank relations. It reduces the number of suppliers of bank services. This can make it harder for treasury managers who currently deal with many banks. Size has some advantages, also. For example, larger banks should be able to expand the number of services they offer in the money markets. This could mean additional suppliers for corporate users.

Conversely, the sheer size of newly merged banks may shrink the market so much that smaller, regional banks can no longer compete with their huge rivals. This could translate into fewer suppliers of basic bank services and, possibly, higher costs as a result. Treasury managers must be prepared for consolidation and have contingency plans developed in case a major bank is no longer able to supply company needs.

Closely related to bank consolidation is national banking. Whether through interstate mergers or the legislative removal of legal prohibitions, national banking appears to be coming. This may not mean much to small, regional corporations, but to companies that operate on a national level with many local units, true national banking would be welcome news.

Having banks with branches (or affiliates) throughout the country could significantly reduce the number of bank relationships companies in certain industries (e.g., fast food, automobile rental, service stations) must now maintain. Being able to deal with fewer banks would greatly improve the treasury management systems of these companies. They would also probably require far less sophisticated field deposit concentration and local disbursement products. National banking would probably have the same effect on the number of providers and on bank costs as bank consolidation would.

Increased pricing and cost pressures

One encouraging sign for banks is the expansion of the corporate market. Bank services, especially traditional cash management services, are no longer just for large companies.

By targeting smaller and middle-market companies, banks have been able to expand the size of the non-credit services market substantially. These parts of the market are also heavy users of bank credit services, so for many banks this has been "the best of both worlds." But, just like their large company colleagues, treasury managers in these smaller firms are becoming better informed consumers and are more demanding of their bank service providers.

Corporate attitudes toward bank services will certainly set the tone for the relationship in the future. For example, the changes in bank compensation methods and the increases in bank charges have brought bank services to the attention of corporate financial management.

As corporate treasury managers have had to justify the costs of bank services, their attitudes toward these services have changed. More and more, services of questionable value or ones with high price tags are being replaced or reduced in use.

This may put a strain on the traditional bank relationship, but it also creates a better working environment. Companies will be more likely to insist on some form of performance measurement in the future, so the banks that are prepared to deal with ways to measure service quality will fare the best.

Finally, the bottom line—the total cost of bank services to the company—will set the framework for the corporate-bank relationship. If this cost gets too high, there will be pressure from inside the company to control its growth and find alternate ways to reduce the operating expense.

This may mean doing more things in-house. For instance, many companies (e.g., utilities, mail order firms) have created their own retail lockboxes internally. They then can reduce bank charges and process orders or payments quickly.

They may also have been encouraged by better electronic services to convert much of the paper payments to electronic ones, using direct debits or "plastic" methods of payment. If other services surpass internal thresholds, banks can expect to see companies establish new in-house services. If costs become a big issue, competition from non-bank vendors may also increase as these providers offer similar services at a savings.

Expanding the market

As banks are allowed to expand into other markets, such as the securities market, and compete head to head with current non-bank vendors (e.g., investment banks, large insurance companies), treasury managers will probably see an expansion in bank marketing efforts. Such an expansion will offer the corporate treasury manager more alternatives for services that banks currently do not provide.

This will not occur overnight, but there could be benefits (e.g., lower prices) for corporations and expanded relations for banks. Several commercial banks have already moved into the commercial paper market, so corporate treasury managers should expect to see new sources for old products.

Banks have also faced stiff competition from non-bank vendors, and there are no signs that this will change. Banks will have to work hard to maintain corporate relationships. Competition from non-bank sources could directly affect corporate-bank relations if non-bank vendors are able to build and maintain a competitive market share.

It is possible that non-bank competition will increase as costs (and, in turn, industry revenues) for bank-supplied services are raised. For corporate treasury managers, more suppliers could mean more competition and, consequently, lower prices. For commercial banks, it may mean stiffer competition from nontraditional sources, and this could mean pressures on profitability.

Continued growth in the small corporate market is probably good news for banks in general. It means more corporate relationships to manage, but it also means continued market growth. Banks that are oriented toward this expanding market segment should enjoy future market successes.

The possibility of shifts in marketing strategies by some major banks may mean less focus and intensity on the large corporate market by the banks and fewer banks to choose among for large companies. This could then place more importance on existing relationships for both sides.

Many large banks have signaled that they intend to concentrate on the smaller end of the market, but they do face substantial competition from the thousands of local community banks that can offer comparable core cash management products and local contacts. For many small businesses, having someone locally as a contact outweighs the perceived benefits from dealing with a larger bank, not to mention the higher costs associated with larger banks.

Maintaining effective corporate relationships is an integral part of the smooth operation of a bank's marketing efforts. Knowing what a customer needs today and is likely to require tomorrow is a prerequisite for successful corporate-bank relations. Banks must work hard to keep up with their corporate customers, large and small. The successful bank is the one that stays on top of things.

Regulatory and legislative events

Regulators and legislators can help or hinder bank relations. In the past, treasury practices that took advantage of weak spots in the payment systems or in the Federal Reserve's system for clearing checks were identified and outlawed by law. Regulators also influence credit services by imposing additional reporting or increased loss reserves for questionable loans. Changes in the FDIC's role have eliminated its *too big to fail* policy that kept several financially troubled banks afloat in the 1970's and 1980's.

Regulators and legislators have helped accelerate the growth in electronic payments, providing enabling legislation that can be used to assist in developing more electronic payments and using feedback from banks and their customers on the potential impact of proposed regulatory change. For example the Check 21 legislation, passed in 2004, can help checks clear faster by permitting banks to make electronic copies of the checks and use these for clearing. While these records are not true ACH items, they are a lot better than the old paper check and can simplify the collection systems of many organizations.

Banks and their customers have shown willingness in the past to work together for the good of both parties. This joint action has provided regulators like the Federal Reserve with better feedback and guidance as the Fed tries to improve its payment processing.

Linking services

During times when interest rates are low and banks make slender returns on unused lines, banks are likely to be dissatisfied with the meager returns and naturally look for additional revenues from their existing customers. In the past many organizations that were consistent borrowers had no trouble lining up the banks needed to provide their short-term credit needs; other services were not so important.

However, with a shift in focus to fee-based income and increased prices for the "other" services as well as a lengthy period of unwelcome small spreads in borrowing rates vs. the bank cost of funds, banks started to ask for additional services to justify offering customers new or renewed credit lines. Without this additional business, no lines would be offered. This problem is more likely to affect larger organizations that need more than one bank to provide all their financing needs. Smaller organizations do not usually need more than their major bank.

There is some question as to the legality of a bank's linking credit availability to other revenues. In the Bank Holding Company Act of 1970, banks were prohibited from "tying" practices—i.e., requiring customers to use additional banking services to obtain the credit lines they desired. The tying prohibition has been interpreted as applying to investment banking services, but its applicability toward cash management and other non-credit services is unclear. What is clear is that there are many treasury managers who are negotiating with banks that are reluctant to offer stand-alone credit facilities.

In its "2004 Credit Access Study" the Association for Financial Professionals reported that 87% of executives from larger companies (annual sales of more than $1 billion) responding to the association's February 2004 survey acknowledged feeling pressure from their bankers to award other business to the banks offering credit. In addition, 63% of executives from large firms reported that during the preceding five years they had been denied credit or changed the terms as a result of the bank's failure to get additional business.

The survey also reported that customers were feeling stronger pressure from their banks in terms of revenue targets they were obligated to meet. Over half of the respondents felt they were unable to meet these targets without giving substantial non-credit business to their banks.

These findings are troubling, to say the least. I think it indicates how seriously banks are looking at their bottom line. I also believe that it clearly marks a change in the way banks and their customers are looking at banking services and relations.

In the past customers may have felt that banks were satisfied with "some" business and tended to use the prospect of further business as a competitive pressure, not a requirement of service offering. If this new focus continues and becomes the norm in the banking world, treasury managers will have to change.

The ability to roll up all your services into one bank may be difficult if you need multiple banks for credit lines. You may be able to work around this by putting revolving credit agreements together, but this is a time-consuming and expensive process. It should be a wake-up call to define your credit and non-credit needs as well as ancillary needs, such as investment banking and financial advisory services.

Where do you go from here?

Bank relations are important to the organization and the treasury manager because banks still provide major financial services. For the organization, this means that it will continue to require a number of sources to supply necessary services if it is to benefit from market competition. It also means that the organization should continue to work closely with its major banks to broaden the knowledge base of employees on both sides.

Continued feedback should result in additional technical improvements and new services. For the treasury manager, bank relations will not decrease in importance. Treasury managers will have to be better educated, better informed, and better prepared to work with their banks to ensure a steady stream of effective products and services.

Maintaining effective bank relations will be important as the banking world undergoes change. Corporate and other organizations are also not immune to change, and the treasury managers will have to be skilled in living with and managing change.

New vendors will undoubtedly emerge. New services will be conceived, and new relationships will be started. Old relationships will end, either voluntarily or involuntarily. Overall, though, those treasury managers who develop effective and flexible approaches will find the future challenging but not impossible to handle.

Chapter 10 ACTION ITEMS

§ Maintain current list of favorites/bookmarks.
Segment your bookmarks by type, such as those
shown in Figure 10-, including:
   • Banks
   • Non-bank financial institutions
   • Link sites
   • Government sites
   • Association sites
   • Publication sites

§ Evaluate imaging applications, such as lockbox
imaging or positive pay imaging. Maintain a
current "position" on the use of imaging by your
company.

§ Identify and maintain a list of all potential
electronic payment applications throughout the
company.

§ Stay abreast of e-commerce and EDI developments
at your company by joining multi-departmental
projects and/or periodically meeting with
marketing and technical managers.

§ Evaluate how much you are currently using or
possibly could use a national bank. If appropriate,
try to match up national bank branch locations
with company sites that handle cash.

Chapter 10 ACTION ITEMS (cont.)

§ Monitor the growth and availability of services in smaller, more community-oriented banks. Periodically determine whether these banks have developed competitively priced services.

§ Along the line of the previous item, identify and monitor progress of any non-bank competition. Regularly evaluate whether the non-bank supplier has anything to offer your company.

§ Identify services or groups of services that could be offered to company credit banks as part of a package to obtain adequate credit services. Periodically revisit this to be sure that the services are being handled properly.

APPENDIX A

Definition of Basic Terms

Account analysis statements	Monthly statement provided by bank to company, showing average balances and service charges for each account and (usually) company summary.
Automated clearing house (ACH)	Place where electronic funds transfer in structions from member institutions (banks and other financial institutions) are ex changed. There are regional ACHs around the country.
Bankers acceptance (BA)	Financial instrument used to finance for eign and domestic trade transactions. It car ries a bank's guarantee to make payment to the holder of the BA at maturity.
Collected balances	Bank account balances after float, or items in the process of being balances collected, are taken out. These may also be called available balances or good funds.

Commercial paper (CP)
: Financial instrument, sold directly or through a dealer in bearer-note form, to finance short-term working capital transactions. CP has a maximum maturity of 270 days.

Compensating balances
: Balances maintained by companies in the form of collected balances in their bank accounts for the purpose of compensating their banks for bank services. Calculated levels of these balances may appear on monthly bank account analysis statements.

Controlled disbursement
: Cash management service offered by banks that includes notification of check clearings by early to mid-morning in time for companies to fund their bank accounts on the same day.

Electronic Data Interchange (EDI)
: The exchange of business transaction information in an electronic medium. EDI uses standard transaction formats and replaces much of the paper invoice processing between trading partners.

Daylight overdraft
: The extension of intra-day credit to banks by the Federal Reserve. The Fed has initiated a program to control the levels of day light overdrafts in the banking system.

Fedwire
: Funds transfer system of the Federal Reserve system. This is an on-line, real-time system offered only to commercial banks. Payments made via this system are immediately available to the receiver.

Fee compensation
: Compensation for bank services by explicit payment by the company to the bank.

Ledger balances	Gross balances in a company's bank ac count, unadjusted for float or items in the process of being collected.
Letter of credit	Borrowing instrument issued by a bank on behalf of its customer (a company). The bank guarantees it will make payment if a specified action or series of actions take place. These are commonly used in international trade and to support short-term borrowing.
Line of credit	A specified amount of funds that a bank agrees to offer its customer (the company), usually over a specified period of time, such as a year, subject to availability from the bank.
Lockbox	Collection service offered by most banks to companies, which involves the bank's receiving customer payments directly (through a P.O. box number), processing and depositing the checks and sending remittance details to the company.
Retail lockbox	Type of collection service characterized by large volumes of checks in small denominations that are usually accompanied by a machine-readable remittance document. These are often consumer-to-corporation payments.
Revolver	Credit agreement between a company and a bank or group of banks for a specified time period. This differs from a "regular" line of credit in that it is a legal contract between borrower and lender(s) and guarantees, subject to the terms of the agreement, that the agreed-upon amount of credit will

	be available during the time period specified.
Target balance	Average daily collected balance a company wishes to maintain at its bank. This is usually set for the bank as a whole and maintained through a master control account.
Treasury work stations	Computer systems used by companies via personal computers for various treasury activities, such as obtaining bank account balance and transaction information, transferring funds electronically and other treasury information.
Wholesale lockbox	Type of collection service characterized by small volumes of checks in large denominations. These are often corporate-to-corporate payments.
Zero balance account (ZBA)	Type of bank account arrangement in which individual operating account balances are maintained at zero balance daily by funding through a master account at the same bank.

APPENDIX B

References and Resources

Books

Bort, Richard, Corporate Cash Management Handbook, RIA, New York, NY (2004 with annual updates)

Hill, Ned C. and William L. Sartoris, Short-Term Financial Management, 3rd edition, Prentice Hall, Englewood Cliffs, NJ (1995)

Maness, Terry S. and John T. Zietlow, Short-Term Financial Management, South-Western College Publications, 2nd edition (2001)

Parkinson, Kenneth L. and Jarl G. Kallberg, Corporate Liquidity, TIS Publishing, Hopewell, NJ

Parkinson, Kenneth L. and Raymond P. Ruzek, How to Prepare RFPs for Treasury Services (3rd edition), TIS Publishing, Hopewell, NJ

Magazines & Newsletters

AFP Exchange
Business Finance
Canadian Treasurer
CFO Magazine
Financial Executive
Leahy Newsletter
Treasury and Risk Management

Web Sites

afponline.org: site for Association for Financial Professionals

businessfinancemag.com: site for Business Finance magazine

cfo.com: site for CFO magazine (note that this magazine also has an additional Web page at cfonet.com)

fbservices.org: site for Federal Reserve Financial Services

fei.org: site for Financial Executives Institute

gtnews.com: wide spectrum of treasury-related articles

oanda.com: site for foreign currency rates

phoenixhecht.com: resource for treasury managers

tmac.ca: Canadian treasury management association

tmpages.com: cover treasury management and related topics

treasuryandrisk.com: site for *Treasury and Risk Management* magazine

Index

Treasury Information Services focuses on cash management, treasury management, and working capital management. It provides consulting, training, and editorial services to corporations, government agencies, and not-for-profit organizations as well as to banks and other service providers. Through TIS Publishing, it publishes books that are widely acknowledged to be insightful, practical, and eminently useful. (See page 184 for information on ordering.)

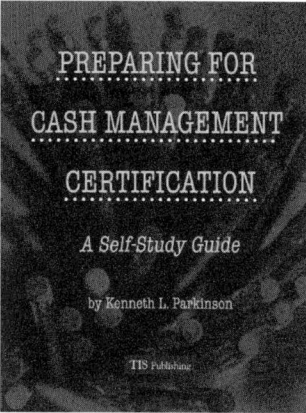

Preparing for Cash Management Certification

This self-study guide includes detailed reviews, test-taking tips, study aids, and more than 300 original practice questions. It is revised and kept up-to- date with the current version of the body of knowledge.

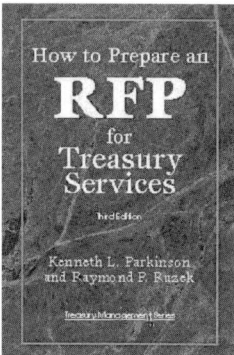

How to Prepare an RFP for Treasury Services

This is the only RFP book written expressly for treasury managers. It discusses how to secure management support for an RFP, how to deal with vendors, how to evaluate responses, and how to managed the RFP process. It also include over 600 questions in 37 separate questionnaires.

TIS Publishing Quick Order Form

Fax orders: 609-466-0091. Send this form.

Telephone orders: Call 1-888-TIS-BOOK (847-2665) toll free.

E-mail orders: books@tisconsulting.com

Postal orders: TIS Publishing, P.O. Box 99, Hopewell, NJ 08525

Please send *Optimizing Bank Relations: Managing Costs and Services* (I understand that I may return my book(s) for a full refund.)

No. of copies _____ x $35.00 per copy = $_____

Please add 6% sales tax for books sent to NJ $_____

Shipping (US): $4.50 for first book and $3.00
for each additional book; **Outside US:** varies $_____

Please send information about:
[ ] Other books [ ] Consulting [ ] Training [ ] Editorial services
Name:_____

Tel:_____ E-mail:_____

Firm:_____ Dept: _____

Street:_____ Mail Code:_____

City:_____ State:_____ ZIP:_____

Payment: [ ] Check enclosed
 Credit card: [ ] MasterCard [ ] Visa [ ] American Express

Card number: _____

Name on card: _____Exp. date:_____

Billing address for card:_____

City:_____ State:_____ ZIP:_____